CHAMPIONS OF FREEDOM

The Ludwig von Mises Lecture Series

CHAMPIONS OF FREEDOM
Volume 21

CAN CAPITALISM COPE? FREE MARKET REFORM IN THE POST-COMMUNIST WORLD

Richard M. Ebeling, Editor

Ronald L. Trowbridge, Executive Editor
Lissa Roche, General Editor

Hillsdale College Press
Hillsdale, Michigan

Hillsdale College Press

Books by the Hillsdale College Press include the *Champions of Freedom* series on economics; *The Christian Vision* series; and other works

CHAMPIONS OF FREEDOM:
CAN CAPITALISM COPE? FREE MARKET REFORM IN THE
POST-COMMUNIST WORLD
© 1994 by the Hillsdale College Press
Hillsdale, Michigan 49242

Printed in the United States

First printing 1994
Library of Congress Catalog Card Number 93-081160
ISBN 0-916308-71-5

Contents

Foreword

For twenty years, America's most distinguished scholars and active decisionmakers have met on the Hillsdale College campus to pay homage to one of the world's greatest champions of freedom, Austrian school economist Ludwig von Mises (1881–1973). Perhaps the College's proudest possession is Mises' personal library. Upon bequeathing the library to us, Professor Mises said he had done so because "Hillsdale, more than any other educational institution, most strongly represents the free market ideas to which I have given my life."

When the history of the twentieth century is written, the Mises name will surely be remembered as that of the foremost economist of our age. Certainly the history of one period during this century ought to include his name writ large: the one in which we are now living, the one that will be forever remembered as the time when the Berlin Wall finally came crashing down. The man who took out the first brick was Ludwig von Mises. He did it with books such as *The Theory of Money and Credit, The Free and Prosperous Commonwealth, Omnipotent Government, Bureaucracy,* and *Human Action.*

Mises based his theory of economics on the supremacy of the individual. The rational, purposeful, day-to-day decisions of ordinary men and women are what constitute the market and are the basis of all human action. It was his understanding of the market as a process, against the background of continually changing conditions and limited individual knowledge, that set his theory so clearly apart from the rigid, mathematical attempts of other economists bent on devising "models" of equilibrium.

Few economists perceived so clearly the consequences of the ideas set in motion by the statist and collectivist mentality. He warned that the greatest danger to Western society would come with the increasing concentration of political and economic power in the hands of the state. He used the example of communism in the Soviet Union and Eastern Europe to point out that the peril was real indeed.

It was Mises who wrote so eloquently and forcefully that the state could never successfully control the marketplace any more than it could control the lives of men. In fact, Mises' testimony convinced prominent Marxist-Leninist intellectuals to admit in the early 1980s, long before the demise of the Soviet Union, that "the world is run by human action, not by human design."

We honor his vision, his courage and his enduring wisdom in this 21st volume of the *Champions of Freedom* series.

Hillsdale College
Hillsdale, Michigan

George Roche
President

Contributors

Elena Bonner, the widow of Nobel scientist Andrei Sakharov and founder of the Sakharov Congress, began her career as a volunteer army nurse in 1941. She graduated from the First Leningrad Medical Institute in 1953 and practiced as a district doctor and pediatrician and as a foreign aid health worker in Iraq.

She became a political dissident in the late 1960s, and in 1970, at the trial of a fellow activist, she met Andrei Sakharov. They were married in 1972. From 1980 to 1986 they lived in Gorky, the city to which Sakharov had been exiled by the Soviet authorities. Elena Bonner's *Alone Together* is a memoir of those years. Since her husband's death in 1989, she has become in her own right one of the leaders in the democratic movement in Russia and has written a second book, *Mothers and Daughters*.

Vladimir Bukovsky is the founder and president of Resistance International, a human rights organization dedicated to the welfare of political dissidents. Upon his arrest in 1963 for possession of literature criticizing elite members of the Communist Party, he was sentenced to a special prison hospital in Leningrad. He would spend eleven of the next thirteen years in Soviet prisons. In 1970 he recounted his experiences in an interview with the *Washington Post*. It was the first time that the psychiatric abuse of Soviet dissidents had appeared in the Western press. In 1971 he was arrested for the final time after his compilation of eight case histories of psychological torture surfaced in Paris.

While in prison, he collaborated with a fellow inmate to write *A Dissident's Guide to Psychiatry,* which was published in the West in 1975. After an intense campaign by international human rights activists, he was released in 1976. Since his emigration, he has maintained an active speaking schedule and written *To Build a Castle: My Life as a Dissenter, The Peace Movement and the Soviet Union,* and *To Choose Freedom.* He is currently at work on a volume about KGB documents he has examined under the new Russian government.

Richard M. Ebeling is the Ludwig von Mises Professor of Economics at Hillsdale College. A former assistant professor at the University of Dallas, he joined the Hillsdale faculty in 1988. In addition, he serves on the editorial board of the *Review of Austrian Economics* and as vice president of the Future of Freedom Foundation.

He is the editor of *Money, Method and the Market Process: Essays by Ludwig von Mises* and a number of volumes in Hillsdale's *Champions of Freedom* series. Professor Ebeling has lectured extensively on privatization and monetary reform throughout the United States and Latin America, and he has traveled to the former Soviet Union on several occasions to consult with the Lithuanian government, the city of Moscow, and the Russian Parliament.

Vitaly A. Naishul is the founder and president of the Institute for the Study of the Russian Economy in Moscow. Formerly, he was a senior research fellow at two organizations within the Academy of Sciences of the U.S.S.R., the Institute of National Economic Forecasting (1986–1993) and the Central Economic-Mathematical Institute (1981–

1986), as well as at the Institute of Economics of the State Planning Committee of the Council of Ministers of the U.S.S.R. (1971–1981).

In 1991, he served as an economic consultant to the newspaper known as *Nezavisimaya,* or "Russian Independent," and as a member of the International Center for Research into Economic Transformations. He is also the author of *The Last and Supreme Stage of Socialism.*

George Roche has served as president of Hillsdale College since 1971. *Firing Line,* the *MacNeil-Lehrer News Hour, Today, Newsweek, Time, Reader's Digest* and the *Wall Street Journal* have chronicled his efforts to keep the College free from federal intrusion. Formerly the presidentially appointed chairman of the National Council on Educational Research, the director of seminars at the Foundation for Economic Education, a professor of history at the Colorado School of Mines, and a U.S. Marine, he is the author of twelve books, including six Conservative Book Club selections, among them: *America by the Throat: The Stranglehold of Federal Bureaucracy , A World Without Heroes: The Modern Tragedy , Going Home, A Reason for Living,* and *One by One: Preserving Freedom and Values in Heartland America.* His most recent book is *The Fall of the Ivory Tower: Government Funding, Corruption, and the Bankrupting of American Higher Education.*

Aleksandras Shtromas is Professor of Political Science at Hillsdale College. He has taught at a wide variety of colleges, including the Universities of Bradford and Salford in Great Britain, the University of Chicago, Boston College and Stanford University's Hoover Institution on War, Revolution and Peace. He has published numerous works, including eleven books on law and politics, and nearly one hundred monographs, articles and book chapters. Titles of recent years are *Political Change and Social Development: The Case of the Soviet Union* and *The End of "Isms"? Reflections on the Fate of Ideological Politics After Communism's Collapse*.

Born in 1931 in then-independent Lithuania, Dr. Shtromas was imprisoned in a Nazi concentration camp during World War II. After the Soviet reoccupation of Lithuania, he studied law at the Universities of Vilnius and Moscow, and he became one of the U.S.S.R.'s leading legal scholars. Dr. Shtromas wrote widely in the official Soviet and East European academic press and also in *samizdat* (underground) publications. Because of his active participation in the dissident movements in Lithuania and Russia, he was persecuted by the Soviet authorities, and he was finally forced to leave the country in 1973.

Aaron Wildavsky (1930–1993) was the Class of 1940 Professor of Political Science and Public Policy at the University of California-Berkeley. The former chairman of the political science department and dean of the graduate school of public policy, he also taught at Yale University, Hebrew University in Jerusalem, and Oberlin College. In addition, he served as the president of the Russell Sage Foundation in New York and as president of the American Political Science Association.

His articles appeared in dozens of sources, including: the *American Political Science Review,* the *American Spectator,* the *Brookings Review, Commentary,* the *Public Interest, Reason, Society,* the *Stanford Law Review,* and the *Southern California Law Review.* He was also the author of nearly thirty books. Among them were: *The Rise of Radical Egalitarianism; The Beleaguered Presidency; The Moral Collapse of Communism: Poland as a Cautionary Tale; How to Limit Government Spending;* and *The Politics of the Budgetary Process.*

Introduction

Communism is the secret name of the dread antagonist setting proletariat rule with all its consequences against the present bourgeois regime. It will be a frightful duel. How will it end? No one knows but gods and goddesses acquainted with the future. We only know this much: Communism, though little discussed now and loitering in hidden garrets on miserable straw pallets, is the dark hero destined for a great, if temporary, role in the modern tragedy.... Wild, gloomy times are roaring toward us.... The future smells of Russian leather, blood, godlessness, and many whippings. I should advise our grandchildren to be born with very thick skins on their backs.

Heinrich Heine (1842)

Socialism—that is the state substituting itself for individual liberty, and growing to be the most terrible of tyrants.

Ledru-Rollin (1848)

Since the beginning of recorded history the state has attempted to control the economic activities of its subjects. Four thousand years ago, the Code of Hammurabi detailed in dozens of laws the prices that merchants could charge for various products and the wages that could be paid for the labor of numerous artisans.[1] The Incas of Peru constructed and ruled a vast collectivist empire in which the state over-

1

saw in meticulous detail the tilling of the soil, the irrigating of the land, the distribution of what was produced and the cultural indoctrination of the people.[2] The Jesuits of Paraguay established communal societies in which land was assigned to families compelled to grow particular crops; villages were erected according to uniform plans, all forms of trade were banned and the produce of the fields was deposited at a public store from which each family drew a portion of the community's output.[3]

In more recent times, the mercantilist system in 17th and 18th century Europe superimposed the regulations of the state over practically every facet of domestic and international trade, with governments specifying the goods that could be produced and sold at home and abroad, decreeing the materials and methods of production with which commodities could be manufactured, and controlling the prices of both raw materials and finished goods and the wages to be paid to the workers who assisted in their production.[4] And the 19th century saw the establishment of numerous voluntary communalist colonies in various parts of America; but most of these attempts to establish collectivist microcosms ended up either as islands of authoritarianism or dissolved away in disputes among the members over the purpose and structures of their communalist paradises.[5]

Even when governments have not attempted or have failed in extending their controls over every corner of social and economic life, there have always been proponents of regimes of comprehensive state power. A defining characteristic of most if not all appeals and apologies for the total state has been the insistence that it is merely a means for the advancement of a greater and more perfect social good. Most of the advocates of what in the 19th and 20th centuries became known as the "socialist" ideal envisioned an all-encompassing political authority which would use its power to remake society into a paradise on earth. If men were to be denied personal liberty, it was to create a higher freedom.

If private property was to be abolished, it was to establish a more just system of common ownership. If men were to be denied the right to speak and write what they desired, it was to give them a more profound knowledge and wisdom. If men were to be treated unequally before the law, it was to assure a fairer social equality for all. If particular individuals had to be put to death, it was to guarantee a better life for all mankind.[6]

But only in our own century did the socialist vision have its chance to be fully tried and implemented. Walter Lippmann summarized the spirit of our century in 1937:

> Throughout the world, in the name of progress, men who call themselves communists, socialists, fascists, nationalists, progressives, and even liberals, are unanimous in holding that government with its instruments of coercion must, by commanding the people how they shall live, direct the course of civilization and fix the shape of things to come.... This is the dogma which all the prevailing dogmas presuppose. This the mold in which are cast the thought and action of the epoch. No other approach to the regulation of human affairs is seriously considered, or is even conceived as possible.... So universal is the dominion of this dogma over the minds of contemporary men that no one is taken seriously as a statesmen or a theorist who does not come forward with proposals to magnify the power of public officials and to extend and multiply their intervention in human affairs.[7]

Twelve years earlier, in 1926, the Italian historian and classical liberal Guglielmo Ferrero explained what this meant for those who now lived under this dogma of dogmas: "[Governments] force people to study, to work, to fight. They no longer let them sleep, they grind them down and fleece them mercilessly in the name ... of progress, of country ... of socialism, of the people.... Multiple names of one and the same duty: to obey, to work, to pay."[8]

Nowhere was this practiced more completely than in the Soviet empire. Nowhere was there a more complete attempt to remake man and society—a total transformation of the social order. And what made this experiment in creating a new man in a new society so diabolical was precisely the fact that many in the first generation of Bolshevik leaders truly believed in what they were doing. In his book on *Soviet Civilization,* Andrei Sinyavsky explains the character of Felix Dzerzhinsky, the first chief of the Cheka, the Soviet secret police:

> He ... loved nature, flowers. He had a poetic temperament. And ... he adored children. In a letter to his sister in 1902, when he was twenty-five and already a confirmed Social Democrat, Dzerzhinsky wrote: "I don't know why it is that I love children more than anyone else.... I could never love a woman as much as I love them, and I don't think I could love my own children more than other people's.... Very often it seems to me that even a mother cannot love them more passionately than I do." This seems incredible: someone who loves children more than anything else and more than anyone else, even a mother, becomes an executioner. But revolutionary ethics are based on such reversals. The purest and most loving person should be the first to kill. He sees this as his sacrifice for children. And children are our future, communism.... [A]ccording to his wife, his dream—dashed by an early death—was to one day trade ... his work as chief Chekist ... and become people's commissar of education, devoted solely to children and youth. Isn't that a wonderful prospect—in the spirit of communist morality—the chief executioner converted into chief educator?! Into the creator of the new man.... And if he loved children

most of all, the thing he hated most of all was prison. He was able to study prisons better than many Bolsheviks and knew them from the inside.... Out of hatred for prison, Dzerzhinsky became the first jailer after the revolution and the founder of a prison system of a kind that history, most likely, had never known. This was not a betrayal of his ideal—the ideal of freedom—but a concrete struggle for that ideal.... You could never suspect this man of sadism, or of self-interest, or even of a special predilection for prison and police work. He did bloody work not out of love for the art but out of hard political necessity, this being the mission entrusted to him by the Party.[9]

It has sometimes been suggested that socialism—particularly in its Marxian variation—can be conceived as a secular religion, in which man having fallen from grace and eaten from the forbidden fruit of alienizing private property, must pass through a period of earthly hardship and tribulation, until a redemptive revolution returns man to a communalist heaven on earth. And through the traverse of man's alienation various prophets cry in the wilderness, until finally a savior comes and leads the chosen people—the proletariat—out of bondage to the promised land of communism.[10] If we keep this imagery before us, it is possible to understand certain aspects of the Soviet experience and its evolution into bureaucratism and the *nomenklatura* system. Our guide for this understanding can be the famous German sociologist, Max Weber, in his analysis of the charismatic leader, the chosen followers of the leader, and the institutionalization of their rule after their successful ascendency to power.

The charismatic, Weber tells us, is one who stands out from the ordinary mass of men because of an element in his personality viewed as superhuman, or supernatural, or at least containing exceptional power or qualities. He is on a mission, because he has been endowed with a particular intellectual spark that enables him to see what other men do not, to understand what the mass of his fellow men fail to comprehend. But his authority, Weber explains, does not come from men acknowledging his powers. His sense of authority and destiny comes from within, knowing that he has a truth that he is to reveal to others and then knowing that truth will result in them being set free; and when they see the rightness of what he knows their following his leadership emerges as the obvious and inevitable.

Surrounding the charismatic is an array of disciples and comrades who are called and chosen:

> The ... group which is subject to charismatic authority is based on an emotional form of communal relationship.... It is ... chosen in terms of the charismatic qualities of its members. The prophet has his disciples.... There is ... a "call" at the instance of the leader on the basis of the charismatic qualification of those he summons.... There is no such thing as a salary or a benefice. Disciples or followers tend to live primarily in a communistic relationship with their leader.... Pure charisma ... disdains and repudiates economic exploitation of the gifts of grace as a source of income, though, to be sure, this often remains more an ideal than a fact.... Support by gifts, sometimes on a grand scale from foundations, even by bribery and grand-scale honoraria, or by begging, constitute the strictly voluntary type of support. On the other hand, "booty," ... whether [extracted] by force or by other means, is the other typical form of charismatic provision of needs.[11]

In the charismatic's circle there exist no external constraints of the type usually associated with, for example, the rule of law. "There is no system of formal rules, of abstract legal principles.... Formally concrete judgments are newly created from case to case.... From a substantive point of view, every charismatic authority would have to subscribe to the proposition, 'It is written..., but I say unto you'.... [T]he leader merely intervenes in general or in individual cases when he considers the members of his staff inadequate to the task with which they have been entrusted."[12]

But once the charismatic and his followers are in power, a transformation soon occurs in their behavior and relationship to the rest of the society. Now it becomes impossible to stand outside of the flow of the mundane affairs of daily life. Indeed, if they do not now immerse themselves in these matters, their power over society would be threatened with disintegration. Slowly, the burning fervor of divine mission and revolutionary comradeship begins to die:

> Only the members of the small group of enthusiastic disciples and followers are prepared to devote their lives purely idealistically to their call. The great majority of disciples and followers will in the long run "make their living" out of their "calling" in a material sense as well.... Hence, the routinization of charisma also takes the form of the appropriation of powers of control and of economic advantages by the followers and disciples, and the regulation of the recruitment of these groups.... The original basis of recruitment is personal charisma. With routinization, the followers or disciples may set up norms for recruitment, in particular involving training or tests of eligibility.... Correspondingly, in a developed political body the vassals, the holders of benefices, or officials are differentiated from the "taxpayers." The former, instead of being "followers" of the leader, become state officials or appointed party officials.... With the process of routinization the charismatic group tends to develop into one of the forms of everyday authority, particularly ... the bureaucratic.[13]

I would suggest that in Max Weber's analysis of the process by which a charismatic revolutionary movement is often transformed into a bureaucratic state, we see the outline of the historical process by which a band of Marxist revolutionaries, convinced that they saw the dictates of history in a way that other mere mortals did not, took upon themselves to be the midwives of that history. They lived lives of underground subversion and communal sharing, under the threat of imprisonment, exile or execution. They instituted a coup to come to power, fought a bloody civil war to ascend to the throne of being dictators over the proletariat in the name of the proletariat, but then found themselves in the position of ruling over a triumphant revolution. And as the ambers of victory cooled the revolutionaries had to turn to the mundane affairs of "building socialism."

But building socialism meant the transformation of society, and transforming society meant watching, controlling and overseeing *everything*. The handful of professional revolutionaries that Lenin insisted was the key to success prior to the revolution could never manage such a gigantic task by themselves. Hence was born the *nomenklatura:* Beginning in 1919, the Party established the procedure of forming lists of positions requiring official appointment and accompanying lists of people who might be eligible candidates to fill those positions, as well as being eligible for promotion to higher positions of authority. And thus was born the new ruling class of socialism.[14]

Ministries needed to be manned, Party positions needed to be filled, nationalized industries and collective farms needed managers assigned to supervise production and see to it that central planning targets were fulfilled, state distribution networks needed to be established, trade unions needed reliable directors, mass media needed editors and reporters to tell the stories about socialism's breakthrough victories in creating a new Soviet Man and his new glorious society.

Who filled the *nomenklatura* positions with which the new order was to rise up from the ashes of the old regime? Theodore Hamerov once summarized the types:

> ... [T]hose joining the revolutionary movement are impelled by a variety of motives, mostly philanthropic in the early years, but increasingly utilitarian.... [F]rom the beginning there are also those who enter the Party in the anticipation of rewards. They believe in the basic principles of the revolution to be sure; they subscribe in a general way to the doctrine of the radical dictatorship. But their public convictions are reinforced by private calculations. The longer the new order is in power the rosier its prospects become, the larger grows the number of those who support it for reasons of expediency. And in fact Party membership does become progressively more remunerative. Considerable prestige can be derived from the position of responsibility, not to mention the advantage of being close to governmental power: more food, better housing, finer clothes, greater comfort. Nor should the improved chances of professional advancement be overlooked. The faithful follower of the regime can expect more rapid promotion not only in the bureaucracy but in industry, agriculture, education, science, and the arts. These considerations increasingly attract to the revolutionary movement members ... who are ... interested in its rewards....[15]

Contrary to the socialist promises of making a new man out of the rubble of the old order, as one new stone after another was put into place and as the socialist economy was constructed, into the cracks between the blocks sprouted once again the universals of human nature: the motives and psychology of self-interested behavior, the search for profitable avenues and opportunities to improve one's own life and that of one's family and friends, the attempt to gain control over scarce resources and commodities so as to take advantage of mutual gains from trade in a world of unsatisfied wants. Since the state declared its ownership over all the means of production, it was not surprising that as the years and then decades went by more and more people came to see membership in the *nomenklatura* and ancillary positions as the path to a more prosperous and pleasant life. In the end, the socialist state did not transform human nature; human nature found ways to use the socialist state for its own ends.

The system of privilege and corruption that Soviet socialism created has been explained by Boris Yeltsin, in his book *Against the Grain:*

> The Kremlin ration, a special allocation of normally unobtainable products, is paid for by the top echelon at half its normal price, and it consists of the highest-quality foods. In Moscow, a total of some forty thousand people enjoy the privilege of these special rations, in various categories of quantity and quality. There are whole sections of GUM—the huge department store that faces the Kremlin across Red Square—closed to the public and specially reserved for the highest of the elite, while for officials a rung or two lower on the ladder there are other special shops. All are called "special": special workshops, special dry cleaners, special polyclinics, special hospitals, special houses, special services. What a cynical use of the word![16]

But the real tragedy of this experience of socialism-in-practice is that many of its terrible consequences—mass killings, the lose of freedom, the abuse of power, the economic inefficiency of central planning—were already understood and warned about long before the Soviet experiment began in Russia in 1917. In 1899, the French social psychologist, Gustave Le Bon, explained that the immediate fate of the nation which shall first see the "triumph of socialism" is that the "people will of course commence by despoiling and then shooting a few thousands of employers, capitalists, and members of the wealthy class.... Intelligence and ability will be replaced by mediocrity. The equality of servitude will be established everywhere.... The state, having successively absorbed all branches of production, 'will be obliged,' as Signor Molinari remarks, 'to subject a portion of the nation to forced labor for the lowest wage; in a word, to establish slavery,' for the cost price of articles produced by the state is necessarily, as we have seen, higher than the cost price of production in private industry. Servitude, misery, and Caesarism are the fatal precipices to which all the roads of the socialists lead.... It will be hell, a terrible hell." And he added, "One nation, at least, will have to suffer it for the instruction of the world. It will be one of those practical lessons which alone can enlighten the nations who are amused with the dreams of happiness displayed before their eyes by the priests of the new faith."[17]

The first of these nations to suffer for the instruction of the world was Russia and the other national and ethnic groups that comprised the Soviet Union. Le Bon's prevision of the shape of socialist things-to-come merely failed to comprehend the magnitude of the tragedy. In his careful and scholarly study, *Lethal Politics: Soviet Genocide and Mass Murder Since 1917*, political scientist R. J. Rummel calculated the human cost of the Soviet experiment:[18]

Periods of Soviet History:	**Deaths:**
The Civil War Period, 1917–1922	3,284,000
The NEP Period, 1923–1928	2,200,000
The Collectivization Period, 1928–1935	11,440,000
The Great Terror Period, 1936–1938	4,345,000
Pre-World War II Period, 1939-June, 1941	5,104,000
World War II Period, 1941–1945	13,053,000
(Excluding War-Related Deaths)	

Post-War and Stalin's Twilight Period, 1945–1953	15,613,000
Post-Stalin Period, 1954–1987	6,872,000
Total for the Soviet Period	61,911,000

For the instruction of the world, nearly *62 million people* were sacrificed on the altar of socialism in the Soviet Union. Yet the destruction of human liberty that the establishment of socialism entailed was clearly understood and explained before World War I. One of the best descriptions of what a socialist future would hold in store was given by the French classical liberal economist, Paul Leroy-Beaulieu, in his book, *Collectivism,* (originally published in 1885—more than thirty years before the Bolshevik Revolution). It is worth quoting at length:

> It is astonishing to see the number of socialist publications which actually claim that their *regime* would secure the development of individual liberty and dignity! How could liberty exist in a society in which everyone would be an employee of the state brigaded in squadrons from which there would be no escape, dependent upon a system of official classification for promotion, and for all the amenities of life!.... The employee (and all would-be employees) would be the slave, not of the state, which is merely an abstraction, but of the politicians who possessed themselves of power. A heavy yoke would be imposed upon all, and since no free printing presses would exist, it would be impossible to obtain publicity for criticism or for grievances without the consent of the government. The press censure exercised in [Czarist] Russia would be liberty itself compared to that which would be the inevitable accompaniment of collectivism. However numerous the dissentients, they would be condemned to silence and subjected to injustice under the *regime;* and a tyranny such has never

been hitherto experienced would close all mouths and bend all necks....[19]

Intellectual liberty would suffer equally. Mental enjoyment requires books; but since the state would be the only printer and the only bookseller, if the administration fell into the hands of pietists, the production and sale of books, except those bearing the impress of the definite form of religion approved by the state, would be prohibited; the human mind would thus be subjected to a yoke more terrible than it has ever known— the practices of Torquemada and of the Inquisition would be mild in comparison.... Again, what would become of art when the work of artists would be subject to the dictation of the directors of production and the state would be the only purchaser?[20]

[I]t is obvious that liberty of domicile could not exist, since for anyone to change his habitation, it would be necessary for him to obtain an order for a new domicile from the state, the sole proprietor. Every privilege has its price which must be paid, and the cost of liberty of choice in domicile is rent. When this exists no longer, and the state provides a house or lodging gratis, the individual would be as closely bound to his domicile as an oyster to its shell....[21]

The destruction of individuality would be the inevitable result of such a system, and the position of the labourer under it would be worse than that of a serf of the middle ages.... If now a workman falls out with his foreman, if he is unpopular and ill-treated by his fellows, he can change situation or adopt another calling; but what resource would he have when all employers but one have disappeared? To change, he would need the authorization of the state as represented by his immediate superior.... [P]ermission could only be obtained as an act of grace, as in the case of a soldier wishing to change his corp. Is it possible to feel any confidence that the officials who would represent the one universal employer would show no favouritism in the distribution of tasks, in the approval or condemnation of work, and in the fixing of wages, or that there would be no tyranny or persecution?.... To have but one employer [the state] for all trades, and in all places, would impose an odious thralldom upon the wage earner, from which there would be no escape....[22]

Again, what dignity could exist in a society when state obligations would be substituted for all moral duties? Parents would no longer direct the bringing up of their children, for whom they would not be responsible, and for whom they would no longer be called upon to make sacrifices, and in their turn children would no longer assist their aged parents. The honour and happiness of family ties, braced by common effort, by dangers encountered with mutual devotion, and by success and misfortunes would cease to exist. Despised and exposed to state competition, then persecuted by contemptuous and arrogant public doles, personal charity would shrink, fade, and finally vanish. No one would any longer have responsibilities or duties towards their fellow; savage egotism would reign, and the effect of socialism, paradoxical as it seems, would be to establish the most ferocious individualism....[23]

How could human progress continue in a society subject to universal constraint and authority? Authority, whatever its source is always slow, pedantic, and a slave to routine.... [A]n immense bureaucracy would be established, and individuals who are exceptional in any way would be shouldered on one side and crushed by its complicated machinery.... To initiate an improvement or develop an invention, it would not suffice to convince a few persons of its advantages: the *vis inertioe* of red-tapism and professional prejudices would have to be overcome; the inventor would have to deal with numerous officials and committees of the administration; in fact, he would have to conciliate the whole bureaucracy! His task would indeed be herculean! In the face of these formidable obstacles, nine-tenths of all useful inventions would be lost, the progress of humanity would be seriously retarded, and the continuous improvement which now goes on in the method of production would cease. . . .[24]

It has now been made clear that collectivism would be unable to provide a satisfactory system of national production; and that the three following consequences would follow on the establishment of this regime:—(1) The suppression of free individual determination of requirements, or in other words, of personal freedom; (2) the absence of any guide for the necessary control of production; and (3) the retardation or complete cessation of industrial and agricultural improvements, which would result from the substitution of bureaucratic pedantry and arbitrary regulations for the elastic and active organism which now exists, and which is the product of individual initiative, of competition, of the freedom of choice of profession, and of private capital.[25]

As just one more example from those who warned of the dangers to be expected from the implementation of socialism, the following passages from Robert Flint's 1908 volume, *Socialism*, are succinct:

The collectivist state would be the sole producer, and every individual would have to take just what it pleased to produce. At present demand rules supply; in the collectivist system supply would rule demand. The state might have the most capricious views as to what people should eat or drink, how they should dress, what books they should read, and the like; and being the sole producer and distributor of meat and drink, the sole manufacturer of cloth and sole tailoring and dressmaking establishment, the sole publisher and supplier of books, individuals would have to submit to all its caprices ... The mere fact, for example, that all printing and publishing would be done by the state could hardly fail to be fatal to the freedom of the press.... The collectivist state would not be likely either to import books adverse to collectivism, nor to treat the production of them by its own subjects as labor worthy of remuneration.... When supply rules demand, and not demand supply, desires must be suppressed or unsatisfied, freedom unknown, and progress impossible.... The whole tendency of collectivism is to replace a resistible capitalism by an irresistible officialism; to make social authority omnipotent and individual wills powerless; to destroy liberty and to establish despotism. Hence, any society which accepts it must find it, instead of a panacea for its evils, a mortal poison.[26]

There are few aspects, therefore, of the socialist experience since the collectivist experiments of the 20th century began during World War I that the critics of socialism did not anticipate and warn against.

Even the attempt by socialism's apologists to shunt aside the arguments against socialism by insisting that what the critic is criticizing is not "real" socialism but a false conception of what a "true" socialist order should be like, was experienced by the opponents of socialism before World War I. In his 1910 volume, *Socialistic Fallacies*, the French journalist and classical liberal Yves Guyot pointed out that:

As soon as you attempt a discussion with socialists, they tell you that "the socialism which you are criticising is not the true one." If you ask them to give you the true one, they are at a loss, thereby proving that, if they are agreed upon the destruction of capitalist society, they do not know what they would substitute for indi-

vidual property, exchange and wages.... No socialist
has succeeded in explaining the conditions for the production, remuneration and distribution of capital in a
collectivist system. No socialist has succeeded in determining the motives for action which individuals would
obey. When pressed for an answer, they allege that human nature will have to be transformed.... Socialistic
policy can only be a policy of ruin and of misery: The
question which it involves is that of free labor actuated
by the motive of profit as against servile labor induced
by coercion. The socialistic ideal is that of slave labor,
convict labor, pauper labor and forced labor—a singu-
lar conception of the dignity of the laborer.... The entire socialistic policy consists in taking away from individuals for oneself and one's friends. When this policy
is practiced by the highwayman in a story with a blun-
derbuss in his hand, it is called robbery, and the highwayman is pursued, captured, tried, and hanged. The
socialists formulate a theory of robbery and call it resti-
tution to the disinherited.... [T]heir system of spolia-
tion ... [i]nstead of leading to the gallows ... leads to
power, honors, position, and wealth.[27]

The socialist experiment in the former Soviet Union and
Eastern European countries has (hopefully) finally reached
its end. Between 1989 and 1991, these countries—first one
and then another—threw off the straight-jacket of Communist Party rule and began the process of establishing the
formal institutions of liberal, democratic societies. The process in each of these countries, however, is far from complete. With ethnic conflicts and nationalistic antagonisms
present almost everywhere individual liberties are far from
secure; basic freedoms of speech and the press still exist on
shaky ground in most of these countries; private property
rights often lack constitutional and legal recognition and
protection; privatization of state enterprises and assets is

incomplete or nonexistent; state ministries and bureaucracies continue to regulate and manipulate the emerging market relationships and market processes; the mentality of the welfare state dominates the thinking of many in politics and in the general society.

The 20th annual Ludwig von Mises Lecture Series, held in April of 1993 on the Hillsdale College campus, was devoted to the problems facing the countries of the former Soviet bloc in establishing classical liberal market economies, especially the problems of the transition from socialism to the market economy in Russia. The participants included Elena Bonner, human rights advocate and widow of Nobel Laureate Andrei Sakarov; Vladimir Bukovsky, long-time Soviet dissident and victim of the gulag; Vitaly Naishul, Russian free-market economist and director of the Institute for the Study of the Russian Economy in Moscow; George Roche, Hillsdale College president, Aleksandras Shtromas, Hillsdale College professor of political science, myself, and the late Aaron Wildavsky, professor of political science at the University of California-Berkeley.

The contributors attempted to explain the nature of the legacy that socialism has left to this part of the world, analyze the current political and economic situation, and propose alternative policies for establishing and securing of functioning market economies and political regimes that would more successfully guarantee human freedom.

Ludwig von Mises, in whose name these lectures are dedicated, was the leading opponent of socialism in the 20th century. From the time of World War I to his death in 1973 at the age of 92, he warned of the danger to human liberty and prosperity presented by all forms of socialism—whether it be Soviet communism, German National Socialism, or Italian fascism. Indeed, in 1920, he was the first critic of socialism to demonstrate that the central planning of a complex economic order was logically impossible and would lead to economic decay and destruction. Less than twenty years after his death, the collapse of the Soviet Union confirmed the validity of what he had argued seventy years earlier at the beginning of the Soviet experiment with socialist central planning.

But the challenge that faces the countries of Eastern Europe and the former Soviet Union is whether they can successfully free themselves not only from the outward forms of the socialist state, but from the socialist mentality that has dominated the intellectual climate in both the East and the West. Only if this is accomplished will any foundations for a free society be permanently secure in these newly noncommunist nations. The purpose of this latest addition to the *Champions of Freedom* series is to offer ideas and suggestions to make those foundations solid.

Hillsdale College

Richard M. Ebeling
Ludwig von Mises Professor
of Economics

Notes

[1]See the price and wage control statutes in the Code of Hammurabi reprinted in Robert L. Schuettinger and Eamonn F. Butler, *Forty Centuries of Wage and Price Controls* (Washington, D. C.: The Heritage Foundation, 1979), 153–154.

[2]See, Louis Baudin, *A Socialist Empire: The Incas of Peru* [1928] (Princeton: D. Van Nostrand Co., Inc., 1961).

[3]Charles Gide, *Communist and Co-Operative Colonies* (London: George G. Harrap & Co., Ltd., 1930), 58- 88.

[4]Eli F. Heckscher, *Mercantilism*, 2 vol. [1931] (New York: The Macmillan Co., revised ed., 1955); J. W. Horrocks, *A Short History of Mercantilism* (New York: Brentano's Publishers, 1924); Philip W. Buck, *The Politics of Mercantilism* (New York: Henry Holt & Co., Inc., 1942).

[5]Charles Nordhoff, *The Communistic Societies of the United States* [1875] (New York: Schocken Books, 1971) and Mary Holloway, *Heavens on*

Earth: Utopian Communities in America, 1680–1880 (New York: Liberty Publishers, 1951).

[6]Igor Shafarevich, *The Socialist Phenomenon* [1975] (New York: Harper & Row, 1980); Alexander Grey, *The Socialist Tradition: Moses to Lenin* [1946] (New York: Harper Torchbooks, 1968); F.J.C. Hearnshaw, *A Survey of Socialism* (London: Macmillan and Co., Ltd., 1929).

[7]Walter Lippmann, *An Inquiry in the Principles of the Good Society* (Boston: Little, Brown and Company, 1937), 3–4.

[8]Guglielmo Ferrero, *Words to the Deaf* (New York: G.P. Putnam, 1926), 70.

[9]Andrei Sinyavsky, *Soviet Civilization: A Cultural History* (New York: Little, Brown and Company, 1990), 127–128.

[10]Cf., Gustave Le Bon, *The Psychology of Socialism* [1899] (New Brunswick: Transaction Books, 1982), 85–103; and Gary North, *Marx's Religion of Revolution* (Nutley, N.J.: Craig Press, 1968).

[11]Max Weber, *The Theory of Social and Economic Organization* [1922] (New York: Oxford University Press, 1947), 358–373.

[12]Ibid., 361–362.

[13]Ibid., 367 & 369.

[14]Geoffrey Hosking, *The First Socialist Society* (Cambridge: Harvard University Press, 1985), 89; Michael Voslensky, *Nomenklatura: The Soviet Ruling Class* (Garden City: Doubleday & Co., Inc., 1984).

[15]Theodore S. Hamerow, *From the Finland Station: The Graying of Revolution in the Twentieth Century* (New York: Basic Books, Inc., 1990), 280–281 & 283.

[16]Boris Yeltsin, *Against the Grain: An Autobiography* (New York: Summit Books, 1990), 159.

[17]Gustave Le Bon, *The Psychology of Socialism* [1899] (New Brunswick: Transaction Books, 1982), 406 & 408.

[18]R.J. Rummel, *Lethal Politics: Soviet Genocide and Mass Murder Since 1917* (New Brunswick: Transaction Books, 1990).

[19]Paul Leroy-Beaulieu, *Collectivism* (London: John Murray, 1908), 326–327.

[20]Ibid., 166–167.

[21]Ibid., 207–208.

[22]Ibid., 208–209.

[23]Ibid., 327.

[24]Ibid., 327–328 & 184.

[25]Ibid., 185.

[26]Robert Flint, *Socialism* (London: Sir Isaac Pitman & Sons, Ltd., 1908), 166–167 & 186.

[27]Yves Guyot, *Socialistic Fallacies* (New York: The Macmillan Co., 1910), x & xvii–xviii.

Richard M. Ebeling

The Inevitability of Capitalism and the Problems of Privatizing the Socialist Economy

Socialism and Its Critics Before the Fall of Communism

Few things capture the intellectual climate of the last one hundred years more than the fact that practically no literature exists on the problems of privatizing a socialist economy. I say "practically" because it is only in the last ten years or so that the issue has even seemed of relevance. During the last half of the 19th century and the first half of the 20th century, discussions about socialism centered on the problems associated with the nationalizing of private property and the implementation of a system of central planning once the state took upon itself the task of managing the economic affairs of a nation. Even the discussions in a number of Western countries after the 1960s concerning the problem of re-privatizing nationalized industries were carried out in the context of selling off a handful of enterprises in an institutional environment that was still generally based on private property and market exchange.

The types of questions debated by the proponents of socialism from the late 19th century on revolved around whether nationalization of industry, agriculture, and trade should be done gradually or all in one go; whether it could be achieved through peaceful democratic means or whether it would require a violent, undemocratic revolution; whether those who had privately owned the means of production should be paid some form of compensation or whether those who had "exploited" their fellow men should receive nothing for surrendering that to which they had no right in the first place; whether some form of limited and small private enterprise should be permitted after the democratic or revolutionary triumph of socialism or whether all the means of production, great and small, should be reduced to departments or branches of the central planning ministries. And until the 1920s and 1930s, there was almost no discussion among socialists about whether central planning was a workable option; it was merely taken for granted.

Among the opponents of socialism, the issues raised concerned the dangers to human liberty that might be expected from a socialist state that would be the monopoly owner of all the means of production, and upon which everyone in the society would be dependent for earning a living; the problems that would arise in terms of a destruction of the incentives to work and produce once the close link between effort and reward that private property created was eliminated in the socialist state; the weakening of moral character and conduct once the socialist state took responsibility to care for all men in all their affairs, in place of the system of self-responsibility closely identified with the market economy; and a fear, already expressed by a few critics of socialism before World War I, that once state central planning replaced the market system of prices and competition the result would be social chaos rather than social order.[1]

The Austrian Economists and the
Unworkability of Central Planning

After the 1920s, the debate between advocates and opponents of socialism shifted to a different plane. In 1920, Austrian economist Ludwig von Mises published his famous article, "Economic Calculation in the Socialist Commonwealth," in which he challenged the socialists to explain how they intended to plan the economic activities of a society once they had done away with private ownership of the means of production.[2] He extended his criticism of central planning two years later in his book, *Socialism, An Economic and Sociological Analysis*.[3]

The gist of Mises' argument was that to use the resources at his disposal rationally under socialism, the central planner would have to know not only the relative demands for finished consumer goods, but the relative values of scarce resources in alternative lines of production. He would have to assure that they were being efficiently allocated and economized in the various production activities to which they could be applied. Otherwise, all production undertaken in a socialist economy would be potentially "suboptimal," in the sense that the planner could have no way of knowing whether he had misallocated the capital and other resources at his command. In a later book, Mises argued that a fully socialized economy—having eliminated all market relationships—would be reduced to a state of "planned chaos."[4]

The market economy solved the problem of efficiently allocating capital and other resources among alternative uses in society through the private ownership of the means of production. Since capital and other resources were privately owned, and private owners had rights over the use and disposal of those means of production, markets existed upon which they could be bought and sold. Entrepreneurs who desired to have use or possession of them for the undertaking of profit-oriented production activities had incentives to appraise, in as judicious a manner possible, what those resources were potentially worth in terms of the market value of the finished consumer goods they could assist in producing. In competing for their purchase or hire against the bids of others, every entrepreneur and all other participants in the exchange process assisted in bringing about the emergence of prices for the means of production. These market prices then assisted each and every entrepreneur in deciding whether a particular commodity was profitable and what least-cost combination of resources should be used to manufacture it. This assured an economy-wide efficient use of the society's resources and a maximizing of the goods most desired by consumers as expressed in the prices they were willing to pay for them.

But under socialism, Mises insisted, such economic calculation for a rational use of resources would be impossible. With no rights to private ownership of the means of production, there would no ability or incentives for making bids or offers to acquire or sell them—since there would be nothing for people to legally buy or sell. With no bids and offers, there were no consummated exchanges, and with no exchanges there were no market-generated prices, and with no prices there was no way to know the true opportunity costs of using those means of production in various ways. As Mises expressed it in his 1927 volume, *Liberalism:* "This is the decisive objection that economics raises against the possibility of a socialist society. It must forgo the intellectual division of labor that consists in the cooperation of all entrepreneurs, landowners, and workers as producers and consumers in the formation of market prices. But without it, rationality, i.e., the possibility of economic calculation, is unthinkable."[5]

In the 1930s and 1940s, Mises' argument was further developed by another Austrian economist, Friedrich A. Hayek. Hayek argued that the socialists had ignored an important aspect of a social system of division of labor: that matching the division of labor was a division of knowledge. If individuals were to successfully and continuously coordinate their economic activities with all the other members of the society, there had to be a way to easily and rapidly disseminate information about changing circumstances so all participants in their respective corners of the market could adjust their own actions to new supply and demand conditions. This dissemination of information throughout the vast reaches of an expanding system of division of labor was an essential function of the price system. But prices could not perform this function unless they were freely established by market competition and therefore, could correctly reflect the continuously changing circumstances of a changing world.

Hayek also emphasized the importance of what he referred to as the special and ever-changing local knowledge of time and place. Decision-makers needed to have the discretionary authority to use resources as they best saw fit, because the supply and demand to which production needed to be constantly adjusted was often of such a type that immediate changes had to be instituted, and the particular nature of the changes and their significance would only be known and understood by the decision-maker on the spot. But if the decision-maker had to first pass along information to the central planning authority and then wait for instructions and approval before instituting any changes, the circumstances to which production needed to be adjusted would have most likely changed once more before the directives had arrived from the planning center.

Again, central planning would be suboptimal in the sense that the adjustments commanded from "the center" would always arrive too late and would never incorporate the subtleties of the circumstances that only those in a particular corner of the market could fully appreciate. The economic order that was most flexible and efficient in enabling a con-

tinuous adjustment to change was one based on private ownership of the means of production, under which the entrepreneur had full rights of using and disposing of the resources under his control.[6]

The socialist response was to surrender one of the fundamental cornerstones of the rationale for socialism, yet at the
same time still claim victory over the type of criticisms made
by Mises and Hayek. Socialists now admitted that a rational
use of society's resources required some indicator of their
relative values. Therefore, there did have to be some
method for assigning prices to those resources so that they
might be efficiently allocated among the various lines of
production. Strict central planning, they conceded, could
not work and was undesirable. Instead, in the socialist economy, state enterprise managers should have the authority
to compete against one another to obtain needed resources
and, like at an auction, the central planning agency would
adjust the prices of those resources to assure balance in the
economy. Of course, having the authority to set the prices
at which their own enterprise managers could obtain resources with which to manufacture goods, meant that the
central planning authority still ultimately determined what
was produced and how. Hence, the new notion of "market
socialism" came into existence and in one leap, the socialists
discarded an idea that had been at the heart of their vision
of the new society to come—a fully centrally planned economy with neither markets nor prices—and claimed to have
defeated the "Austrian challenge" at the same time.[7]

The Austrian reply was to argue that a centrally planning
agency assigning prices to resources did not make them *real
prices,* and bestowing wider degrees of discretion upon state
enterprise managers would not transform them into market-oriented entrepreneurs. A central planning agency setting the prices at which capital and resources might be obtained by state enterprises was not the same thing as a real
market on which capital and resources could be bought and

sold by private entrepreneurs and investors risking their own money, guided by their own judgments concerning the value of those means of production in an anticipated profit-making enterprise for the satisfaction of actual consumer demands, and in which the entrepreneurial risk-taker was the residual claimant of any profits earned if the enterprise turned out to be successful. As Mises expressed it, "A socialist system with a market and market prices is as self-contradictory as is the notion of a triangular square."[8]

It is a peculiar fact that in the eyes of most economists, the socialists were viewed as the victors in this debate. Many were convinced that while socialism might be rejected for political or moral reasons, as an economic system it was "workable." And how did economists know this? First, many economists were under the spell of mathematical and statistical model building; they believed that with the right quantitative methods and a large enough data base, an economy could be, if not completely planned, at least directed into desirable paths by various governmental policy tools.[9] Also, there were the countries of the Eastern bloc and the Soviet Union. The extent to which Western economists took these nations' statistics and claimed economic achievements at face value cannot be underestimated.[10] And there were those who believed that a form of "market socialism" was demonstrated as a viable option from the experience of the Yugoslavian economy, in spite of studies demonstrating the exact opposite.[11] For those who were either socialists or at least sympathetic to "alternatives" to a market economy, no thought was given to the problems of privatizing a socialist economy because the need or the desirability for such a radical policy change never entered their heads.

The Failure of Socialism and the Problem of Creating a Market Economy

But what about the critics of socialism? For the opponents of socialism in the late 19th and early 20th century, the task they set for themselves was to prevent socialism from being put into practice and to save private ownership and the market economy from the destruction they feared would follow from the institution of central planning—and which all their analyses foresaw with almost clairvoyant clarity. The opponents of socialism from the 1920s and 1930s on, however, failed to give any attention to the problems of how to privatize a nationalized and centrally planned economy. Why? First, I think it is because they were still thinking primarily of the dangers from further extensions of socialism in the West and were thus trying to hold back the growing tide of state planning.

Second, for all the rigor and logic of their own arguments about the ultimate irrationality and unworkability of socialist central planning, I think that most believed (perhaps, unconsciously) that Soviet military might in the post-World War II period and the internal dictatorial power of the Soviet state meant that any such transformation into a market economy would only happen at some time in the far future. The actual timing of the collapse of the Soviet system was not predicted by them—or, for that matter, by hardly anyone else.

Third, Austrian School economists, in particular, were suspicious of all attempts to construct society according to an overarching design. They always emphasized that most of what we call society and the social order—the legal, political, cultural and economic institutions—are the cumulative, unintended outcome of generations of human actors pursuing their various individual and group ends; and, through their actions and interactions, these multitudes of individuals generated—to use Hayek's favorite quotation from the

18th Scottish philosopher Adam Ferguson—institutions and arrangements "which are indeed the result of human action, but not the execution of any human design."[12] Sudha Shenoy, a loyal follower of Hayek's view of society as a spontaneous order of mostly unintended outcomes of societal and historical development, has argued, "The rule of exchange, and the rules of private case-law, can emerge only as people act accordingly.... " That is, rules of exchange and the principles of contract law can only emerge out of the process of markets beginning to function and with the institutions of a successful market order only slowly emerging and taking various shapes out of the process of continuous trade and exchange. But:

> For such a price network to develop, direct and organized economic relationships need to be established among firms. In the Eastern European context, this means that government must be eliminated altogether from the production process: government must make no attempt to direct production or prices, and there must be no government ownership of resources. Therefore, the extent to which a catallaxy [a market order] emerged would depend on how far rules of exchange and private case-law were in fact developed through the actions of the people themselves. This is the only method of establishing a market order and private law. Government no more creates the catallaxy [the market order] and privately-evolved legal rules than it creates a language.[13]

For markets to emerge, for prices to be formed, for commercial institutions to develop, it is necessary for objects to be traded. That is, there must be private ownership of the means of production and an ability to freely buy and sell the resources with which commodities are manufactured as well as the finished goods themselves. The first task, therefore, must be to privatize the economy, so as to create the precondition upon which markets, prices, and commercial institutions can arise. A fundamental difficulty with most discussions concerning the establishment of an explicit and legal market order out of the rubble created by the socialist catastrophe is that these discussions have presupposed that under socialism-in-practice no property rights have existed, and that markets and prices have not already been functioning in these socialist systems. But, in fact, this has not been the case, as a look at Russia reveals.

The Nature of Market Relationships
under Soviet Socialism

Fifty years ago, the German economist, Walter Eucken, constructed a categorization of different types of economic systems. He pointed out that there were two pure types: First was the centrally planned economy, in which all things down to the smallest detail were commanded by the central planning agency. Everyone, in all their assigned tasks, was required to obey and follow the instructions from the center. Second was the exchange economy in which the state was strictly limited to the protection of life and property. All decisions concerning what was to be produced, what methods were to be used and to whom producers were to sell their output was determined solely on the basis of free exchange among the community participants.

But within these two extremes were a variety of conceivable types of systems representing partial planning and partial exchange, with history producing many of these hybrids depending upon the political and economic evolution and developments in different countries. Within the exchange economy, for example, Eucken argued that one could create two subclassifications: an open and a closed market. A market was open "if every individual or group, has access to the market as supplier and demander, and if each individual

can supply and demand whatever quantity he thinks fit." A
market was closed "when access to the market as supplier
and demander is not open to everyone, for example, when
only a particular closed circle of entrepreneurs can supply
or purchase from a particular market, or when there are
vetoes on construction and investment, or when only a particular group of workers is permitted to work at certain jobs,
or when only a particular group of households may buy
particular goods."[14]

The Soviet Union was never a pure command or planned
economy, even during the height of the Stalinist era. This
was the case for two reasons. First, even during the most
repressive years under Stalin, there existed a flourishing
black market.[15] The reason for this is obvious.[16] Whenever
the state either prohibits the selling of certain products or
sets prices below what the market would have established,
there have always emerged illegal markets to satisfy the frustrated demands of consumers. In the Soviet Union, consumer demand was frustrated for practically everything.
The inherent inefficiency of central planning and the interest of the state in allocating resources into those channels
representing the goals of the Party authorities, rather than
for the fulfilling of consumer demand, resulted in shortages
of practically all the commodities demanded in ordinary
daily life. It was inevitable that corruption would develop
in every corner of the production and distribution process
in the socialist economy, as those who were willing to take
the risks would bribe and blackmail wherever and whenever
necessary to gain access to commodities that others desired,
and for which a higher price could be received than was
charged in the state retail stores.[17]

Russian economist and former dissident Lev Timofeyev
has explained the reasons for and the nature of the black
market that emerged in the former Soviet Union:

For the three-quarters of a century that the Communists ruled Russia they did everything to destroy the ordinary relationships of buying and selling—at least in the production sphere—and replace them entirely with centralized planning and distribution of resources. But the living needs of people, the common sense of society, and the demands of production just did not coincide with the plans and orders of the Communist bureaucrats. Therefore, even though it was strictly prohibited, the black market flourished even under the threat of jail and the death penalty; and in doing so, it preserved market relationships, enabling them to profoundly and triumphantly to penetrate the entire system of the socialist economy.[18]

In other words, the pure planned economy was undermined by the attempt of ordinary people to fulfill those ends the satisfaction of which was prevented because the allocation of resources and the distribution of goods and services according to state command was inconsistent with the desires of the actual producers and consumers in the society. Hence, the Soviet planned economy had a parallel market upon which resources were illegally appropriated, prices agreed upon, and exchanges made.

But there was also a second dimension to the Soviet black market, one that was unique to the Soviet-type economy. This second dimension has also been described by Timofeyev:

One of the peculiarities of the black market [in the Soviet Union] is that, because there is no private property, the merchant sells goods that don't belong to him, and the buyer does not become the owner of what he buys. Whether it is cotton or a car, pipes or paper, or land, timber, irrigation systems, farms, or factories, they do not belong to local Party officials or ministers or the chairmen of collective farms. But what does be-

long to them is full discretionary power over these
riches, just as in fact they have power over the people
who produce these riches. The power itself to control
goods is bought and sold. And authority is the ultimate
good on the Soviet black market. The "commodity of
power" is the most expensive commodity but the most
profitable.... [T]he special feature of the [Soviet] black
market is not so much the material valuables that circu-
late as the power to *allocate* these valuables. On the black
market, the actual rubles do not purchase an automobile, a tractor, or a steam engine but only the *right* to
come to a distributor's organization and arrange the
purchase of the good from the state. We pay the cash
to the person who has the power to allocate the item
we need.[19]

Timofeyev asks, "Is this a bribe? Yes, it is a bribe. But a
bribe, among other definitions, in our situation is also a
special instrument by balancing price in accordance with
supply and demand. It is an instrument through which an
additional permission fee is brought into the price, a fee
permitting the circumvention of existing restrictions."[20]

Every conceivable "commodity of power" finally came to
be for sale in the Soviet Union. One could pay, for example,
to become the rector of a university or one of the senior
personnel in the admissions department at an institution of
higher learning. And large sums would be paid to have control or influence over the admission and graduation process
at such an institution. Why? Because those in charge then
possessed that discretionary power over allocation of a
scarce resource—in this case, a seat in the school. In 1979,
the required bribe for university admission in Leningrad
and Moscow was estimated to be in the range of 3,000 to
5,000 rubles—large sums at that time. In Soviet Georgia, the
price for acceptance into medical school was 15,000 rubles;
and in Baku, Azerbaijan, entry into the Economics Institute

cost 35,000 rubles.[21] Even Party positions were for sale. In a Central Asian Soviet Republic, for example, one could become a regional Party secretary for a ruble bribe equivalent to $150,000.[22]

Russian economist Vitaly Naishul has argued that as this system of "buying" power spread throughout the Soviet economy in the post-Stalin period and reached its highest development during Brezhnev's regime, the textbook conception of a command-economy no longer applied in the Soviet Union. The system of directives from the top down, to which all were required to be obedient, had slowly and in a totally unplanned way been replaced by a system of bureaucratic market relationships. The more complex the economic relationships and links in the production and distribution processes, the more the outcome depended upon the cooperation of each decision-maker and manager at every step of the production and distribution process. The "purchase" of a position of power was paid for not only with cash but with loyalty to those who had assisted an individual in attaining his rank in the hierarchy of control over the allocation of resources and commodities. Tribute was paid to those above, and tribute was received from those below in the hierarchical chain of the central planning structure.

But tribute paid and received in cash, favors, privileges, and loyalty meant that decisions required understandings, compromises, agreements, and a consensus among those in the various hierarchical chains of the planning structures. Paying tribute in these various forms and expectations that participation in the planning process increasingly required degrees of approval by each participant in the hierarchical chain and produced implicit beliefs that what one had "bought" was a "property right" over the use and disposal of the resources under one's control. These were property rights not in law—something unthinkable in the socialist society—but in mutual understanding among those in the hierarchical chain.[23]

There existed in the Soviet planned economy, therefore, several interdependent market economies. It was one of those particular hybrid economic types—partial command and partial exchange—of which Walter Eucken wrote. There was the bureaucratic market in which positions of power over the allocation and distribution of scarce resources were bought and sold in the currencies of loyalty, bribes, and privileges. There was the black market in which, either with or without the consent of the bureaucratic "property owners," resources and commodities were "transferred" from the control of state facilities to the hands of private individuals who then resold them illegally to those willing to pay the highest price. And there was the market between state enterprises; invariably state enterprise managers would find that the centrally allocated supply of raw materials and resources necessary to fulfill the assigned production quota was insufficient to produce the required output, or that they were left with inventories of raw materials and resources in excess of the minimum required to fulfill the production quota. State enterprises created markets between themselves to either barter away excess or acquire deficient supplies of the factors of production.[24] Each of these markets had their bargaining methods, pricing techniques, and institutional procedures for transacting business.

But all of these markets in the Soviet system were what Eucken called "closed markets," i.e., entry was limited into them on the basis of Party affiliation, personal connections and risk of imprisonment. But most of all, entry was limited precisely because property could not be legally acquired and owned by private individuals. As a result, each of these markets had characteristics usually associated in economic theory with either monopolies or cartels. Access to bureaucratic and state enterprise power over the allocation and distribution of some portion of the means of production meant the ability to obtain monetary and nonmonetary profits in excess of those that would have been earned if the markets for resources and commodities had been private, open, and competitive.

It is this factor more than any other that explains much of the resistance to change in the Soviet-type economies since the formal demise of the communist systems in Eastern Europe and the former Soviet Union.[25] The bureaucratic and ministerial positions in the successor governments to the communist regimes—often still manned by many of the same people as before—are the source of continuing political profits, through the power to issue export and import licenses, approve property leases, guarantee the provision of certain essential supplies or materials. Freeing the economy from regulatory procedures and licensing requirements would sink these political profits to zero, since market participants would no longer need these state approvals to go about their production and exchange activities.[26]

At the same time, the resistance to change at the enterprise level can be explained for similar reasons. State enterprises under socialism have operated under what the Hungarian economist Janos Kornai has called the "soft budget constraint."[27] Unlike a private firm in a market economy which must operate within the confines of its own limited financial resources and economize its expenditures within the context of the changing cost and price conditions of the market, state enterprises under socialism have been able to stay afloat with subsidies allocated from "the center," or by receiving cheap credits from the central bank, or from legally fixed prices for both inputs and their own output, or from assured state-allocated supplies of raw materials required for various production activities and state purchases of the goods they have manufactured. The shift to a free market means the arrival of a "hard" budget constraint and the loss of guaranteed political profits. It then becomes sink or swim on the basis of private market capability.

The Process of Privatization in the New Russia

Formal privatization has been occurring against the background of this resistance to change. The wild corruption and often unscrupulous wheeling and dealing in Russia today is part of the final drive of the political profiteers to grab as much as they can while the political grabbing is good. But the fundamental controversy surrounding formal privatization concerns the question, to whom shall the formal and official property titles be passed? The Russian government's privatization program that was set in motion in the fall of 1992 works under the assumption that the property belongs to the state and that it may disperse it among the population on the basis of its own view of equity and efficiency.

In August, 1992, at the time of the first anniversary of the failed coup-attempt that set the stage for the formal end of the Soviet Union, the official privatization program was announced by Boris Yeltsin. He informed the Russian people that effective October 1, the government would begin issuing "investment vouchers" (or "privatization checks") with which shares in companies could be bought as state enterprises were placed on the auction block during 1993. Every man, woman, and child born before September 1, 1992 would be eligible to receive a voucher with a face value of 10,000 rubles. They could be used to buy shares directly or could be invested in mutual funds being formed on the market, or could be sold on the market for cash.[28]

State enterprises, it was explained, would be privatized under one of three options. The first option gives an enterprise's employees non-voting shares equal to 25 percent of equity for free. The employees can purchase an additional 10 percent of equity at a 30 percent discount of book value. Senior managers of the enterprise can purchase up to 5 percent of equity at book value. Under the second option, employees can purchase 51 percent of the firm's shares at book value if two-thirds of the firm's employees vote in favor of this alternative. They are allowed to pay only half of the shares with vouchers, the other half must be paid in cash. With the third option, employees can purchase 20 percent of equity completely in vouchers at a 30 percent discount in the form of a one-year lease contract basis, during which time reorganization with outside specialists must be set in motion to establish the firm on a profitable basis. All remaining shares not purchased by the management or workers under these three options are then to be sold at public auction.[29]

This method of privatization ignores the arrangements that had evolved under the socialist system, i.e., the system of bureaucratic "property rights" upon which market and exchange relationships had developed under socialism. Having "bought" a bureaucratic "property right" in the Soviet era, these purchasers and holders of allocational power have been trying, in the dawning capitalist era, to transfer their "ownership" into formal private property rights in the new Russia. Russians have come to call this process "*nomenklatura* privatization" or "wild privatization." And it appears that to a great extent these "wild privatizers" have been successful.

Even before the privatization plan was officially announced, complaints were already being made that the long delay in privatizing state enterprises had resulted, in the words of former Moscow mayor Gavrill Popov, in the meat having been removed, with only the bones left.[30] He was referring to the fact that in an increasing number of those state enterprises that were profitable or had a high probability of becoming profitable, the top managers and many workers had already taken advantage of transforming their firms into private joint-stock companies with themselves as the shareholders.

In September, 1992, after studying the way enterprises

were planning to privatize themselves under the voucher plan, economist Vasily Selyunin concluded that shares equivalent to only 33 percent of state property would end up being available for purchase by the general Russian public, not the 90 percent claimed by Anatoli Chubais, chairman of the State Property Committee responsible for privatization. And he suggested that at the end of the privatization process large portions of the shares of many privatized firms would remain in the hands of the state.[31] Free market economist Larisa Piyasheva argued that, on average, 60 percent of the property in the country could remain in state hands, with the state maintaining a significant controlling interest in large numbers of "privatized" firms. "Enterprises in which the state still holds a share of the capital are mixed enterprises, part private and part state-owned," Piyasheva said. "They will not operate according to the laws of the market." She considered this to be "an outright deception of the public."[32] And in fact, while hundreds of state enterprises are indeed being placed on the auction block, the majority of the shares in each of these enterprises are remaining in the hands of the management and workers of the enterprises in question, and in the hands of the state as a residual minority shareholder, or, in a large number of cases, with the state as the majority shareholder.[33]

Piyasheva has suggested that the outcome of this particular privatization process in Russia will be

> some kind of strange economy the likes of which probably exists nowhere in the world. A mixed economy in which neither state nor private enterprises exist (unlike any Western economy), but an economy in which every enterprise is partly private and partly state.... These enterprises cannot be ruined, in the classical sense, like private enterprises in a market economy (because some of the shares are in state holding companies that will

keep these enterprises afloat). . . . At the same time, they are not state enterprises.[34]

Now does it matter into whose hands the state property initially falls? In the long-run, in a market economy, it does not. Regardless of how the property is initially distributed, over a period of time the market will itself redistribute it. In a competitive market the only way in which an owner of the means of production can maintain or increase his control over that property is to apply it in ways that ultimately satisfy the demands of the consuming public. His failure to do so results in losses that, if not corrected, finally leads to bankruptcy and the selling of the assets he has owned. These assets then pass into the hands of those who are willing to bid for their purchase—with the expectation that they can use them in more profitable ways than the original owners. Within a few years the distribution of property titles generated by the market's test of entrepreneurial competency will be noticeably different from the distribution of those property titles at the beginning of the process.

If the privatization is undertaken on the basis of vouchers, as it is being undertaken now in Russia, some voucher holders will use them to buy into the ownership of the enterprises placed up for auction. Others will be fearful of the uncertainty and risks arising from being an investor, and they will choose to sell their vouchers for a certain specific sum of money in the present. Others will want to purchase the vouchers being sold so as to be able to buy larger blocks of shares in various firms for the purpose and in the hope of earning larger returns in particular enterprises or to gain enough shares for a controlling interest in a firm and thus to have the power to directly influence the enterprise's activities. This is already going on in Russia today. But having large blocks of voting shares does not assure that investors will have the business acumen to guarantee profits, and if they fail in this task, share prices will fall, and others will eventually take over control of the enterprise.

If privatization follows the path of "*nomenklatura* privatization*," the end result will still be the same. Having had the ability to be political entrepreneurs in the Soviet system—with the business acumen of knowing how to capture political profits—does not mean that those same individuals will have the expertise to transform themselves into market entrepreneurs capable of winning profits in an open, competitive market. Those who are unable to make this transformation will experience losses rather than profits, and property titles will again change hands over time, with the means of production being controlled by those who are able to pass the market test of competitive competency.

In terms of short-run efficiency between these two methods of privatization the *nomenklatura* form is probably the preferable one. It enables a transition to a normal market with a higher degree of continuity and possibly greater stability, since those who are given the legal property titles initially are the ones already possessing the local and specific knowledge of how and with whom to enter into normal exchange relationships in the vertical and horizontal structures of the economy in particular sectors of the market.

Political Regimes and the Market Order
After Privatization

The problem, from the long-run economic point-of-view, is not how to formally privatize, but the political regime in which it is occurring. At the present time in post-Soviet Russia, the political regime is still not clearly defined and is in a state of flux. As this volume goes to press, the broad consensus among most leading political and intellectual leaders and the general public within Russia is for a democratic regime rather than an authoritarian one. The points of dispute concern questions about the structure and division of powers under a new constitution; the degree to which political authority and decision-making powers will be delegated to the various regions, republics, and provinces within Russia; and what powers and responsibilities will reside with the central authority in Moscow.

In practice, nobody and everybody currently seems to possess political authority in Russia. Every level of government passes decrees, laws, and directives and every one obeys or ignores those decrees, laws, and directives—including the central and regional governments themselves—depending upon whether they find them conducive and in harmony with what they want to do, regardless of what the various political authorities publicly declare to be their goals, intentions, and orders. When a Russian businessman was asked what he thought would happen with the implementation of a value-added tax, he replied:

> VAT? Nobody's going to pay it, at least not what they owe. The smaller companies are the best off, because the smaller the company, the easier it is to evade taxes. Bigger ones need advertising, for instance, which attracts attention. As for the tax police: Sure, they will have a lot of competent professionals, and certainly they will catch some people. But the country is very large, and the tax police are very small. Not to mention that they will immediately be corrupted—in this country, every source of control is a source of corruption, by nature. And it doesn't matter how big their computer for tracking hard currency transactions will be. Most of these transactions are under the table: twenty times more hard currency is illegally traded than legally. The most common way of avoiding being tracked is that money is simply credited to bank accounts out-

side the country. It is impossible to track all movements of money.[35]

The enforcement of contracts and property rights have even been "privatized," with some business activity operating in a twilight world of private armies and police, and a violent settling of conflicts and disputes. "It is not only gangsters who resort to weapons during score-settling," Russian journalist Igor Baronovsky explained in May of 1993:

> The accumulated firepower is being employed more and more often by seemingly respectable businessmen as a last argument in settling property and financial disputes. An illustration of this is the wave of violence that has swept Moscow offices.... To be successful today it is no longer necessary to strain one's brain and to devise complicated commercial combinations; you send a few well-armed "fighters" to your rival and thus secure a contract that would be to your advantage. In the same way you can solve problems concerning the renting of apartments, acquiring sites for construction, and getting credits.[36]

Only with the approval and implementation of a new constitution will private property fully and formally come into existence. And Russia is still waiting for a market-oriented code of contract law. Meanwhile, Russian and Western businessmen who desire to do business in Russia must function in an environment of bribery, corruption, bureaucratic and underworld mafias, broken promises, and an inconvertible currency.[37] The various cities and regions of Russia follow different paths towards market-type reform and privatization. Some cities and regions delay, retard, or attempt to reverse the reforms already introduced, while in other places in Russia the majority of small retail stores and enterprises have already been privatized, and Russians enjoy the pleasures of consumer-oriented salesmen attempting to attract their business. In many of the rural areas, on the other hand, the system of production and retail trade is the same as it was before Gorbachev.

One experiment in radical reform began in April of 1993, with the election of Kirsan Ilyumzhinov as president of Kalmykia, an autonomous republic in southern Russia bordering on the Caspian Sea. A self-made multimillionaire (in dollars, not rubles), he ran his campaign on the promise of a major shift to a market economy and won supporters by giving out millions of dollars in money, goods, and food from his own personal financial resources. "Under the present tough conditions, no one is under any obligation to feed us, and besides, it is shameful to rely on charity. We have to learn to earn our own living and to gear our appetites to our pocketbooks. Pinning our hopes on the customary subsidies means perpetuating the republics' backwardness and encouraging dependence," Ilyumzhinov insisted during the campaign. "Organizational and legal conditions will be created for the development of private property and entrepreneurship, with equal protection of all forms of property. Private property is sacred and inviolable. It is necessary to start up this 'perpetual motor' of civilization, which functions successfully in countries with a market economy...."[38] He was insistent that "soon the world will start talking about the Kalmyk miracle. Our state will take off, thanks to the creation of a tax-abatement zone within its territory. Capital will stream in." However, Ilyumzhinov's defense of political and civil liberty was less strong than his belief in the freedom of the market: "All parties and movements will be banned—temporarily, until our standard of living is twice the Russian level. There is nothing to hold rallies about—we must work. And not for five days a week, but six—so that we don't grow weak. Women shouldn't work at all; let them stay home and raise children. I will close

virtually all local newspapers—they only hinder reform...."[39]

A week after taking office as president of Kalmykia,
Ilyumzhinov disbanded the Supreme Soviet (the republic's
parliament) saying that a new parliament would be elected,
comprised of only 25 professional economists and lawyers,
in place of the previous 130 deputies. He restructured 40
government ministries into five smaller ones, with most of
the 40 simply abolished. He shut down the local KGB, seal-
ing its premises and began an audit of its files and records.
"He abolished all district administrative structures, putting
all state farm directors directly under himself and appoint-
ing them personally. He gave political parties a scare, promising to shut them all down and get rid of them until the
complete victory of capitalism. But he didn't shut them
down. Instead, he bought them off in a most original and
curious way. 'Are we going to continue blathering, or are
we going to do something?' he asked, advising them to become—guess what?—commercial enterprises, and offering
them start-up capital from his own lordly fortune," a Russian correspondent reported. And, Ilyumzhinov declared,
"We don't need borders and customs checkpoints; let our
neighbors fence themselves off from us.... Kalmykia should
become one single commercial firm that will earn its own
living. Let at least one republic stop standing outside the
Kremlin walls with outstretched hands."[40]

But besides the problems of privatization and market-oriented reform, the monetary situation in the former Soviet
Union has been in a state of chaos since 1992. Price inflation
was in the double-digit range almost every month and continued during the first half of 1993. After a price-inflation
rate of about 2,500 percent for 1992, the price-inflation rate
was still soaring at a 1,100 percent annual rate during the
first five months of 1993.[41] During the first six months of
1993, the ruble fell in value more than one hundred percent

against the dollar, from 415 rubles to the dollar in January, to 1,102 rubles to the dollar in the middle of June.[42] Civil wars are being fought around the fringes of Russia in a number of the newly independent states that were part of the old Soviet Union. Some fear that ethnic conflict will spread to the territory of Russia and might even threaten to bring about the territorial disintegration of the Russian Federation.

Nobody has a crystal ball, and Russia's history has been dominated by one political tragedy after another. But unless catastrophe strikes, Russia will probably slowly put its political house in order. A more stable, clearly delineated constitutional political regime will finally take shape. Civil society will continue to progress and envelop more of normal, everyday life. The crises that the nation may, and probably will, pass through will be many, but Russia will find its way to a much more normal and civilized social order.

And Russia will probably have some form of a functioning and legal market economy. But what type of market economy? To what extent will the market be open, competitive, and free of government regulation, control, and intervention? What will the monetary system be like? And what will be the established fiscal policy? To what extent will the state continue to have controlling or influencing interests in the enterprises that are and will be privatized? Will the market be open to international trade, or will there be significant trade barriers and protectionist policies? The answers to these questions will be crucial for determining the results that will follow in the wake of the privatization processes occurring in the Russian economy.

A likely shape of Russia's future market order can be traced out based on the views of some prominent intellectuals, economists, and political authorities. When the establishment of a free market in Russia is talked about by Russians, what they usually mean is that they desire to see Russia have a market economy like those they see in Western countries today. They take the existing economic systems of the United States and Western Europe as the standard by which they judge where Russia should be in terms of market institutions and what the role of government should be in the economy.

For example, in February, 1993, a delegation of Russian businessmen, government officials, and economists attended the annual World Economic Forum held in Davos, Switzerland to interact with prominent businessmen, government officials, and economists from most of the leading countries of the world. Among the Russian participants was Sergei Stankevich, one of Boris Yeltsin's leading advisors. "The most important thing I tried to clarify for myself was how world politicians and entrepreneurs saw the state's role in the economy," Stankevich told Russian reporters at the end of the forum. "In recent years, the idea that the state must quit the sphere of the economy as soon as possible has gained the upper hand in my country. However, the main figures at the Davos forum spoke about the opposite—about the state's considerable intervention in the economy and about industrial policy. The need for this was insisted on by Akio Morita, chairman of the Sony Corp., members of Bill Clinton's new economic team, and spokesmen for European, notably, German companies."[43] The lesson that Sergei Stankevich went home with is that what Russia should emulate—if it is to follow the methods of what passes for accepted economic policy in the West—is not unregulated free markets, but the state-managed market economy in which the government plays a prominent and sometimes dominant role in directing, subsidizing, and assisting private enterprises both in domestic and international markets. This is what he learned from the "best and the brightest" in the political, intellectual, and business communities of the West.[44]

In early April of 1993, at a political roundtable (on measures to overcome the economic crisis in Russia), organized by the Russian Parliament and government, academician L. Abalkin, on behalf of four institutes of the Russian Academy of Science, presented a document outlining an anti-crisis program. Russian economic journalist Otto Latsis reported:

> The draft proposes that "the bulk of monetary resources be concentrated on the state program for 'Conversion of the Military-Industrial Complex,' so that through that program, many other high-priority problems of structural reform, including the problems of food, housing, construction, etc., can be resolved." To protect Russian goods producers, it proposes that the idea of "hastily opening up the domestic market" be abandoned. It contains many proposals for the regulation of prices, including the assertion that the state "can and should regulate prices in keeping with consistent technological transformations of the economy." The draft suggests that the state budget deficit be "temporarily" maintained at its present level [approximately 20 percent of Russian Gross National Product] and the state debt be increased. It proposes to "ease the tax bite," immediately issue credits to agricultural enterprises, compensate the population for at least 70 percent of the increase in prices [which could only be done by printing even more money], raise the percentage of the budget expenditures for health care, education, science, and culture, and implement many other costly ideas.[45]

And as Otto Latsis concluded, "To sum up, one could say that, on the whole, this draft is a fairly logical description of the system of bureaucratized anarchy that destroyed even the once mighty economy of the U.S.S.R. This set of ideas could finish off the barely functioning Russian economy in a matter of days, if the government dared to implement it."[46]

A few days after the April 25 referendum, Boris Yeltsin

delivered an address before the Russian Federation Council
of Ministers. He said that the most important result of the
referendum was "The Russians people's support for the policy of profound, radical transformation that the president
and the government have been pursuing since 1992." And
Yeltsin went on, "We are obliged to take the most resolute
measures to achieve the goal of our economic transformation—*the formation of a socially oriented market economy.*" The
Russian president emphasized the importance of complet-
ing the privatization process, the transference of federal
land to the hands of private farmers and owners, the stabilization of the ruble, and the sustaining of an anti-inflation
policy.

But he also said, "Special attention must be paid to the
problem of growing unemployment. We have to work out
employment guarantees for employees of state enterprises
that are declared bankrupt for the period of their financial
recovery. We must immediately begin work on creating a
state system, and providing incentives for private systems,
of vocational retraining for the unemployed and job place-
ment for them in priority branches of the economy. It is
time to set about organizing public works programs, especially in the spheres of housing construction and road construction," and he proposed government insurance and
government funding programs to support new private entrepreneurial activity.[47]

At the same meeting of the Russian Federation Council
of Ministers, Prime Minister Victor Chernomyrdin delivered a report on the state of the Russian economy and presented an outline of the directions for economic policy for
the rest of 1993. Chernomyrdin explained that, "First of all,
the social orientation of economic policy is being strengthened.... Following the adoption of decisions on the establishment of the latest minimum wage, wage rates have twice
been raised in the budget-finance sphere [i.e, for all workers
still employed in the state sector]. The pay of servicemen

and rank-and-file command personnel of internal affairs [the security and the secret police] has been raised twice, as have the benefits for children and cost-of-living adjustments. Pensions and minimum pension levels were increased as of May 1, 1993, and the social problems of undergraduate and graduate students were also not forgotten [stipends for students attending schools of higher learning were significantly increased].... Pensioners, families with many children and single-parent families will be given assistance not only in the form of cash payments, but through the provision of a minimum amount of vitally necessary goods and services at reasonable prices [i.e., at continued state-subsidized prices]."[48] The prime minister also explained that state policy was to regulate wages in the sectors still under government control: "Unjustified discrepancies in the level of pay in the [resource] extracting and [oil] refining industries, as well as between individual regions, have to be corrected."[49]

Thus what both Yeltsin and Chernomyrdin see as the necessary, desirable, and required steps towards continuing "market reform" is the continuance and reinforcement of the welfare state. This is what is being meant by instituting a "socially-oriented market economy." But the "socially-oriented market economy" for the new Russia does not end with the welfare state. The new Russian economy, as conceived by many in the present Russian government would be one guided by a National Industrial Policy—i.e., the rebirth of state planning under the label of market-oriented reform. Russian economic journalist Mikhail Berger has commented that under the leadership of the Ministry of Economics, preparation has begun of:

> draft plans for the state's influence on the country's social and economic development—indicative plans.... The ministry also wants to determine state structural and innovational [sic] policy for the country as a whole

and by regions; basic guidelines for investment policy including the enlistment of foreign capital; federal social policy, including an incomes policy; price-formation policy, foreign economic policy.... It is envisaged that this plan will include a plan for allocating targeted capital investments, a plan for granting tax breaks, a plan for granting quotas, licenses, and special dispensations involving foreign currency and customs, a plan for centralized measures relating to prices and incomes policy—in short, a list too long to give in full....[50]

Indeed, the proposals floating about and being seriously considered are for the privatization of large enterprises not as independent, competitive firms, but as large vertically integrated cartels with the support and assistance of the state. Furthermore, the state is being proposed as the financial subsidizer of science and technology and industrial development. Minister of Foreign Economic Relations Sergei Glazyev, a proponent of a new Russian National Industrial Planning system, has argued that the realization of Russian industrial and technological potential requires "intricate cooperation among hundreds of enterprises, research institutes and governmental departments.... In order to ensure this coordination, it is necessary to form an interdepartmental council [in the government] on industrial policy that would include the heads of the relevant departments. This council would be expected to ensure, on a systematic basis, coordination between the goals of long-term industrial policy, on the one hand, and policy in the fields of privatization, defense, and foreign-economic activity, on the other, as well as allocation of budgetary appropriations for state purchases and investments...."[51]

In the present climate of political and economic opinion, therefore, what the new Russia is moving towards is not a free market economy, but an economic order with partly privatized market relationships upon which will be superimposed the Western world's version of the interventionist welfare state, with elements of a resuscitated planned economy. Perhaps in the ideological and intellectual climate in both Russia and in the wider world today, this is the best for which we can hope. For the fact is that in the West as well as in the new Russia, very few understand what a really free society and a free economy mean, or why they are both desirable and essential for the long-term preservation of liberty and prosperity. Intellectuals around the world still are beguiled by the social democratic illusion that individual freedom can be maintained and sustained without any significant loss of anything "really important," while at the same time the state intrudes and interferes into the economic affairs and social relationships of the citizenry. Most intellectuals and political thinkers still do not believe that infringements on economic liberty and freedom of association constitute steps on a road leading to variations upon the socialist theme.[52] Thus Russia seems to be choosing a path with road signs that point the way from Soviet communism to something in between democratic socialism and the interventionist welfare state.

But this also means that the outcomes resulting from the process of privatization will be influenced in various ways by the manner in which the property titles are initially distributed among the members of Russian society. The very purpose of government intervention in economic relationships is to deflect them from the form and pattern they would have taken if the state had limited itself to the role of protector of private property rights and adjudicator of contractual disputes.[53] This also means that individuals, who potentially will be impacted upon by these policies in either positive or negative ways, have incentives to participate in the political process to assure that the interventions rebound to their advantage, or at least do not impose burdens or losses on them greater than those that might have naturally occurred through the normal sequence of events in the market.

If the state takes upon itself the role of redistributor of wealth, subsidizer of exports or production, protector from competition, or supporter of various types of industrial and agricultural development, then profits and losses, market shares, and relative income earnings are partly or totally the result of the play of politics. In the Russian setting, those who can manipulate the privatization process to assure that they are the initial recipients of private property endowments are then placed in a stronger position to play the political game and to bend the results of economic policy into channels that may enable them to maintain what they have acquired through privatization. They can then continue to reap political profits from connections, deals, and bribery with those who will possess the governmental authority to limit competition and to protect the already established private owners of the means of production and enterprises. This explains the emergence of political lobbying by an increasing number of private entrepreneurs in Russia today as a way to fight the use of political power by the *nomenklatura* and to bend state policy toward their own preferred directions—sometimes to merely assure that the market will be more open and less politically hindered, but also to use the state for their own anti-competitive ends.[54]

The Conclusion to the Transformation to the Market Economy

Writing before World War I, Professor Robert Flint of the University of Edinburgh explained why socialism in practice would fail as an economic system:

> As has often been indicated, no council of the wisest men in London, although invested with absolute pow-

ers, could feed, clothe, lodge, and employ the population of that city, were no man allowed to act without their authority, were no competition permitted in buying and selling, and were wages and prices prohibited, and some strictly rational determination of what labor was to receive and what commodities were to be exchanged for, adopted instead. The problem involved is of a kind which cannot be solved by the reasoning and calculation, legislation and administration, even of the wisest and most uncontrolled rulers: it can only be solved, as it actually is solved, by leaving men free, each to seek his own interest and to attend to his own business, to carry his services or his goods where the rise of wages or of prices shows that they are most wanted, and to withhold them where the fall of wages or of prices warns him that the market is overstocked. Even when this method of freedom and of nature is followed numerous mistakes will occur, but they will be comparatively slight, and those of one man will counteract those of another.... But let the collectivist method be tried, and the risk of mistakes will be immensely increased, the provisions which nature has made for their correction will be prevented from operating, the amount of mischief produced by each error will be vastly multiplied, and the faculties and activities of the individuals composing society will be but feebly brought into exercise. It is not only a single city, however, but entire nations, like Great Britain, which collectivists propose to organize on this plan. May we not safely conclude that what they dream of as organization would be ruinous disorganization?[55]

Also before World War I, the French liberal economist Paul Leroy-Beaulieu explained why it was that if a centrally planned socialist economy was established—even one with a system of comprehensive controls and severe punishments for any violation of the planning commands—it would not be able to prevent the reemergence of market relationships:

> The law cannot suppress transactions which social organizations of all kinds encourage and of which human reason approves.... Again, in defiance of all possible regulations, inequality would reappear in the form of private trade. Although all purchases would legally have to be made in the national shops [state-run retail stores], and no person would be permitted to buy goods from his neighbor, it is certain that the more energetic members of society, with the connivance of the more inert, would in the long run establish a complete system of illicit trade. How would it be possible to prevent an economical person ... who foresaw that certain goods were likely to rise in price, from buying them, and selling them when the expected rise occurred at a price somewhat lower than that charged in the national shops.... However severe the regulations might be, it would be impossible to suppress this private commerce. Thus, in a contraband trade in goods, in secret loans ... at interest, and in the large payments which eminent specialists could exact, there would be three potent causes which would soon lead to the re-establishment of inequality of social conditions.[56]

Critics of socialism like Robert Flint and Paul Leroy-Beaulieu understood the impossibility of the planned economy. Years before the first great experiment began in Russia they predicted the events that would unfold. These events have now been lived through by tens of millions of people in the former Soviet bloc. Very few any longer can deny the obvious: There is no viable alternative to a system of market relationships. The question that remains open is, what type of market relationships? Shall it be a market order in which the state is mostly limited to the protection and enforcement of private property rights, and in which decisions about production, pricing, and exchange are left in the hands of those who own, sell, hire, and buy finished commodities and the means of production? Or will it be a form of the state-managed and manipulated economy, in which a significant proportion of economic decision-making continues to be either under the direct control or under indirect influence of the political authority?

Some argue that being concerned about a revival of state-management or manipulation of economic relationships in Russia and other former communist countries is tilting at windmills. No one in the arenas of production and exchange believes in or obeys the state. The state is ignored or gotten around by the emerging private sector in the former Soviet Union. The state is impotent, and when it tries to be intrusive the most that a private agent may have to do is buy someone off to be left alone—a mere inconvenient addition to the private sector's costs of doing business.

But the present anarchy of the political order is itself part of the transition period in the process of moving toward a more ordered civil and political regime. Because the totalitarian state attempted to be omnipresent in every corner of the society, the collapse of the Soviet system has thrown all the political, social, and economic structures into a state of flux. An alternative civil society and social order has been and is emerging.[57] And a more ordered political regime will eventually emerge as well. But the shape and content of this new political regime in Russia will not arise independent of the ideological climate of the time in which it occurs. Indeed, it will reflect it.

At the moment, when Russia is escaping from its communist past, it is easy to focus attention on the dramatic changes going on at the present time: the privatization of small, medium and large enterprises, the emergence of private farming, the growth in consumer-oriented production and sales, the multiplication of retail stores and shops filled with both the necessities and the luxuries of life after seven decades of deprivation and oppression. At the end of 1992, there were 160,000 private family farms; by June, 1993, the number of private family farms had increased to 243,000, with an additional 13,000 private farmers starting up business every month.[58] By May, 1993, 1,339 enterprises had been sold off through vouchers at privatization auctions, with several hundred additional firms placed on the auction block every month.[59] These new private enterprises and the state enterprises that have become joint-stock companies that are to be auctioned off, are developing alternative connections and relationships with each other outside of the old state-distribution networks. All of this is real and really means something. Russia is slowly becoming a normal society—even with all of the other outward appearances of abnormality, i.e., crime, corruption, and confusion. But beyond the escape from communism, there is also the issue of what Russia will look like politically and economically in five or ten or fifteen years, when this period of transition is further along or at its end. The ideological and political ideas of our time will shape and influence that Russian future.

And the prevailing ideology of the last decade of the twentieth century all around the world remains that of the interventionist welfare state. The strict and comprehensive planned economy is unworkable and politically undesirable, it is generally argued, but so is an unhampered, unregulated free market economy. The belief in a "third way" or "middle way" remains the political mirage for which most intellectuals and politicians continue to search on the horizon.[60] Thus it seems most likely that in the coming years, after escaping from the grip of the totalitarian state and the centrally planned economy, the people of Eastern Europe and the former Soviet Union will now follow a path that merely leads to different forms of statism—admittedly far less oppressive ones—than the one they have endured for more than half a century.

December 20, 1993 Postscript: The Direction of Economic Reform in Russia After the Abolition of the Parliament in October and the Voting of December 12, 1993

Once again the world has recently watched as Russia has gone through another of the internal convulsions that has followed in the wake of the ideological demise of communism and the political end of the Soviet Union. If the world stood transfixed for three days in August, 1991 during the hard-line coup-attempt against Gorbachev and his policy of *perestroika,*[61] for two weeks beginning on September 21, 1993 the world was mesmerized after Boris Yeltsin abolished the Soviet-period Supreme Soviet (or Parliament) and declared that nation-wide elections for a new Parliament would be held on December 12.

But the old-line communists, nationalists, fascists, and statists refused to pass peacefully into history; instead, they declared that Yeltsin was no longer president of Russia and appointed Russian Vice President Alexander Rutskoi to that post. For thirteen days, a stand-off existed between the two competing centers of political authority until October 3, when a large demonstration of pro-Parliament supporters broke through the cordon of police around the Parliament. In the euphoria of the moment, Rutskoi and Parliament Chairman Ruslan Khasbulatov sent the mob of "Red and Brown" communists-nationalists-fascists to attack other government buildings, including the state-owned television center. For twelve hours, violence, chaos, and uncertainty reigned in the Russian capital, and the fate of the country hung in the balance.[62] The final act occurred when the Russian military finally responded to Yeltsin's appeals and orders and surrounded the Parliament and had the tank units fire salvo after salvo of cannon shells into the building.

On October 4, the parliamentary defenders finally surrendered, and their leaders were led away to imprisonment, while the Russian "White House" burned uncontrollably, its facade badly charred, blackened, and broken.[63] While the assessments after the destruction of the Parliament were mixed, with many of the most liberal voices who had long supported Yeltsin and his reform attempts now highly critical of his solution of the conflict between the executive and legislative branches, there was hope by some that something good might still come out of the violence.[64] If the death and destruction of those days actually led to democratic elections for a new Parliament and the presidency, as Yeltsin had promised; if the ratification of a new constitution was secured; if the Russian political environment was normalized and stabilized; if a new federal structure could be established between the center in Moscow and the various regions and ethnic republics comprising the Russian Federation; if the nationalist and ethnic strife that was consuming various parts of the former Soviet Union around Russia did not spread into Russia itself. . . . If these "if"s occurred, Russia would have succeeded in relegating the Soviet epoch to the dustbin of history.

But, unfortunately, soon after the violent days of early October suspicions began to emerge about the degree to which a democratic process would be followed or was even possible.[65] Having promised on September 23 that new presidential elections would be held on June 12, Boris Yeltsin reversed himself and announced on November 6 that he intended to stay in office until the formal completion of his term in June, 1996.[66] But then on November 15, Yeltsin reversed himself, again, saying that presidential elections might still be on for June, 1994.[67] Then after the new constitution was passed by referendum on December 12, Nikolai Ryabov, chairman of the electoral commission, said that the vote on the constitution was also a vote of confidence in the president, and thus Boris Yeltsin should serve out his full term in office until June, 1996.[68]

After first stating that the upper house of the new Parliament, known as the Federal Assembly, would be made up of the administrative heads and leadership of the regional councils of the various provinces and ethnic republics that comprise the Russian Federation, Yeltsin then announced that the local councils and regional councils (or Soviets) were to disband and new elections held; while at the same time, Yeltsin said that the upper house of the Federal Assembly would be chosen by direct election by the people.[69] And after endorsing a draft of the new constitution during the summer of 1993 which recognized the "sovereignty" and special status of the various ethnic republics of the Russian Federation, the revised constitution voted on by referendum on December 12 reduced their position to that of the ordinary provinces of the country.[70]

There also were concerns expressed about the amount of access the various parties and voting blocs had to media outlets leading up to the elections, since the electronic media remained in the monopoly hands of the state and so many of the newspapers were dependent upon the state for financial subsidies for their existence.[71] And since the various individuals, parties, and blocs had to spend the month following the events October 3-4 collecting voters' signatures so as to be eligible for official registration for ballot status, all the participants in the elections had only a month for making their respective cases to the public for the actual voting on December 12.[72] The fact that most of these parties and voting blocs had no consistent platforms or political philosophies upon which to present their case to the public and instead tried to attract votes on the basis of high-profile political figures at the top of their candidate lists was another matter that raised concerns about the results that would follow from the elections.[73] Furthermore, those parties and candidates closely identifying themselves with Yeltsin's actions in October campaigned in a complacent manner, believing that they were assured of a pro-reform majority with the defeat of the hard-liners in the old Parliament.[74] On the other hand, the opponents of reform organized themselves, particularly in the rural areas and industrial centers outside of Moscow and St. Petersburg, and played up the fears and doubts of those among the voters experiencing the short-run difficulties of post-socialist adjustment before the appearance of any of the intermediate and longer-run benefits of a shift to a freer market economy.[75]

As a result, the election appeared to create an outcome the opposite of that for which Yeltsin and his supporters had hoped. The last publicly released opinion poll, on December 3, claimed that the pro-reform parties and voting blocs would gain a majority of the seats for the half of the State Duma (the lower house of the new Parliament) elected according to party or bloc affiliation.[76] A week before the election, private pollsters working for Yeltsin told him that the anti-reform forces—especially the nationalist-neofascist Liberal Democratic Party headed by Vladimir Zhirinovsky—were picking up momentum and could be expected to make dramatic gains on December 12.[77] But by then it was too late to significantly influence the course of events.

The results were seen as a disaster.[78] Zhirinovsky's party, according to the preliminary results released on December 14, had won 24 percent of the vote.[79] The Communist Party won 11 percent; the Women of Russia, 8.7 percent; the Agrarian Party, 8 percent; and the Democratic Party of Russia, 5.5 percent. All these parties were considered moderately to extremely hostile to free-market reforms. Their total vote came to more than 57 percent. The only parties representing a public commitment to fuller privatization and more market-oriented reforms that succeeded in gaining enough votes to win seats in the State Duma were: Russia's Choice, with 15 percent; the Yavlinsky-Boldyrev-Lukin bloc, 7 percent; and the Party of Russian Unity and Concord, 5.7 percent. Their total came to slightly over 25 percent.

Preliminary results for the other half of the Duma, or lower house of the Parliament, in which deputies have been elected on the basis of running as individual candidates rather than on party or bloc affiliation, suggests that the Liberal Democrats will not be the largest grouping. While running as individual candidates, many of those people running for these seats indicated an orientation towards or support for one of the parties and blocs participating in the election. When the results from the vote for parties or blocs are combined with the stated party orientation of the individually elected candidates the actual distribution of seats in the Duma will likely result in Russia's Choice having the largest number. As of December 16, the distribution of deputies in the new Parliament was, so far (with all the votes in all the electoral districts not yet counted): Russia's Choice, 94 seats; Liberal Democratic Party, 78; Communist Party, 64; Agrarian Party, 55; Yavlinsky-Boldyrev-Lukin, 28; Independent Deputies, 27; and Women of Russia, 24.[80]

Even if several of the parties hostile to the Liberal Democrats were to form a voting coalition in the new Parliament in opposition to the nationalist-neofascist deputies, deep compromises in the form and content of further steps towards a freer economy in Russia are likely to be expected. All of the parties and blocs, other than Russia's Choice, have argued that the pace of reform has been too rapid and that insufficient "social protections" have been provided for various groups in the society during the transition from the old Soviet system. Several of the larger parties, such as the Communist Party and the Agrarian Party, have strongly criticized the degree of privatization undertaken so far. And even leading members of Russia's Choice, during the election campaign, argued that the "social safety net" needed to be extended and reinforced. As a consequence, the new Parliament will be filled with deputies pressuring for a delays in market reform and calling for more welfare statist legislation, as well as arguing for regulations and protections to shelter various special interest groups from both domestic and international competition.

The problem is that even before these new hurdles emerged, the reform process was following a tortuous path. Throughout the summer of 1993, the battle over economic policy had raged on in Russia. While attention often was focused upon the conflict between the executive branch and the Supreme Soviet (the end result of which was the abolition of the legislative branch by Yeltsin on September 21,) the same conflict went on within the government. The Minister of Economics, Oleg Lobov, the architect of a new national economic planning for Russia, was finally removed in the middle of September and replaced by former Prime Minister Yegor Gaidar.[81] This was meant to reflect a shift back by Yeltsin to a more market-oriented posture towards economic reform.

But the new constitution confirmed in the December referendum enshrines the fundamental premises of the welfare state. Indeed, redistribution of wealth and social guarantees by the state are elevated to constitutional rights.[82] The new constitution contains all the social(ist) provisions that Yeltsin proposed in his original draft in the spring of 1993: The state shall be constitutionally bound to provide retirement pensions; financial assistance for all those threatened with income levels below an official poverty line; public housing to assure that all in Russia have a place to live; a guaranteed minimum wage; protection from unemployment; state-provided medical care; and state-provided education.[83]

At the same time, privatization in Russia continued to rapidly replace the comprehensively state-owned economy during the summer and fall of 1993.[84] A new group of market entrepreneurs has arisen out of the class of former state enterprise managers, the underworld of the black market, and from out of the mass of ordinary people. By the middle of the summer in 1993, at least 20 to 25 percent of the Russian work force was employed in the more than 60,000 privatized enterprises.[85] From the time vouchers were issued in October, 1992 and enterprises began being officially auctioned to September 10, 1993, 4,314 state-owned enterprises have sold shares at auction; these firms employ an estimated four million workers. But out of the authorized stock issuances assigned to these auctioned firms, on average only about twenty-five percent have been sold to the public; the rest has been acquired by the workers and managers of the respective enterprises or have been reserved off the market in the hands of the state.[86] Each month, now, between 300 to 600 of Russia's state enterprises are being sold off at auctions.[87]

And by presidential decree at the end of October, 1993, the process was begun to privatize the ownership of the state and collective farms.[88] But once again, it appears that the method chosen is one that can be used by the collective farm managers—the rural *nomenklatura*—to manipulate the privatization process for their own advantage. Furthermore, there remain restrictions on the ability of both Russian non-farmers to buy into agricultural land open to privatization and foreign investment participation in privatized agriculture.[89]

In principle, it would not matter in the long-run how all these enterprises were privatized in a free market. If those into whose hand the firms first passed were found over time to be poor entrepreneurs or less competent business decision-makers than others, the market through the mechanism of profit and loss and the resulting fluctuations in share prices, would redistribute ownership from one group of hands to another. In five years, for example, the pattern of asset ownership would look significantly different from the initial endowments resulting from the privatization process. But this formation of market relationships and market participants out of the rubble of the former Soviet system has occurred in the context of the existing Russian state structures. At the end of August, 1993, Aleksandr Kotenkov, director of the State Legal Affairs Administration and a member of the Interdepartmental Commission on Combating Corruption, said in an interview: "[O]nly to the uninitiated do the President's [Yeltsin's] team and the Speaker's [Khasbulatov's] team appear to be totally unconnected. Very often, political opposites provide cover for one and the same middle-level figure, and through that figure they are linked to the commercial structures. From the rostrum, they hurl all kinds of charges at each other, but look—they are eating out of the same pot."[90]

That is, privatization in Russia has occurred in the context of political connections, bribery, state-private arrangements, and partnerships. When the approaching end of the Soviet period became clear to more and more of the people who had been part of the ruling apparatus of the system, they began the process of converting that over which they had bureaucratic proprietorship into their own formal private property—and they have succeeded masterfully to a great extent.[91] While hurling attacks against each other from the pulpits of political power, they have been busy using and abusing the system over which they still have had power to grab while the grabbing has been good; their fights have often had less to do with ideological differences and more to do with who would expropriate the state property first and assure a continuance of the streams of state spending in their own, now privatized, direction.

As an increasing portion of the economy has been and is being shifted into private hands, the next stage in Russia's political economic transformation has been developing. The "social market economy" is the covering term, the ideological superstructure—to use a Marxian phrase—to rationalize the fact that many of the new private owners have not had to face the winds of a truly free market, in which open, unregulated competition would determine whether they remained the proprietors of what they had acquired by now satisfying the consumers on the market better than their rivals. By keeping the state as a minority or majority shareholder in their enterprises, many of these new Russian entrepreneurs hope to be able to use the rationale of "the public interest" and "the general welfare" to assure that any losses suffered or profits not honestly earned on the market will be provided from the coffers of the government. Through references to maintaining Russia's "great power" status in the world economy, some of these new Russian businessmen will rationalize their calls for protection from foreign competition and foreign investment that might undermine their market share in an arena of free competition. Under the slogan of "a social safety net," many in the state ministries and bureaucracies hope to justify the continuation of their jobs, budgets, influence, and power. And by appeals to social justice and a concern for the needy and the poor, some in the new political parties imagine that they will have the means to garner votes and win the support of special interests in the new economy and of remnants of the old economic structures.

Only an analyst with an extremely clear crystal ball can see the path that Russia's political future will take over the coming months and years. One can hope that Russia's dark past of tyranny, mass murder, and totalitarian collectivism is finally gone forever. Russia's people have suffered enough in our century. They deserve a better tomorrow. However, a complete break with their past will only be made if they turn away from a road that will merely take them to a different form of economic collectivism: the interventionist welfare state. It would be less brutal and cruel than the Soviet-style collectivism they have known, but it would still leave their lives heavily politicized and open to manipulation by the state.[92]

Yet the interventionist welfare state, as well as elements of existing forms of economic collectivism, seem the most likely outcome of the parliamentary elections of December

12 in Russia. What the last few years in Russia and the other countries attempting to escape from their socialist past has demonstrated is that the destructive effects of political and economic collectivism have been greater than initially believed. The degree to which the state mismanaged the economy has resulted in practically everyone in these societies having to make dramatic changes and adjustments in their lives. And no matter how much people may have come to hate the Soviet system, the change to a new civil society has turned out to be traumatic for many. Even those who have successfully shifted into private sector activities find it difficult to accept an economic environment in which their personal fortunes are dependent upon their own efforts and the changing currents of market circumstances. And as a consequence, having more or less escaped from the monopoly power and privileges of the Communist Party, they are now drawn to secure new monopoly powers and privileges for themselves through the democratic process.[93]

The discomfort and confusion, and the desire to use political means to create artificial harbors of social security and economic protection, serve therefore as the rationales for resisting and opposing more radical market reforms. But as *The Economist* correctly expressed it: "The problem at present is too little reform, not too much.... Russian voters believe they have already endured two years of shock therapy, because that is what most of their political leaders have been telling them."[94] What Russia needs right now are clear voices that can explain why what has been happening so far is the result of only going part of the way towards a real market economy, and mostly in a politically twisted way, and that what is now promised to them by both "moderate" interventionist-welfare statists and "extremist" nationalists and collectivists will only put them back on a road that is better left untrodden.

Notes

[1]See, Richard M. Ebeling, "Economic Calculation under Socialism: Ludwig von Mises and His Predecessors," in *The Meaning of Ludwig von Mises,* ed. by Jeff Herbener (Norwell, Mass.: Kluwer Academic Press, 1993), 56–101.

[2]Ludwig von Mises, "Economic Calculation in the Socialist Common-wealth," [1920] in *Collectivist Economic Planning* ed. by F. A. Hayek (London: George Routledge & Sons, Ltd., 1935), 87–130.

[3]Ludwig von Mises, *Socialism, An Economic and Sociological Analysis* [1922; revised eds., 1936, 1951] (Indianapolis: Liberty Classics, 1981).

[4]Ludwig von Mises, *Planned Chaos* (New York: The Foundation for Economic Education, 1947).

[5]Ludwig von Mises, *Liberalism* [1927] (Irvington-on-Hudson, N.Y.: The Foundation for Economic Education, 1985), 75.

[6]Friedrich A. Hayek, *Individualism and Economic Order* (Chicago: University of Chicago Press, 1948), 77–91 & 119–208.

[7]Oskar Lange, *On the Economic Theory of Socialism* [1938] (New York: McGraw-Hill Book Co., 1964); R. L Hall, *The Economic System in a Socialist State* [1937] (New York: Russell & Russell, 1967); H. D. Dickinson, *Economics of Socialism* (London: Oxford University Press, 1939).

[8]Ludwig von Mises, *Human Action, A Treatise on Economics* [1949] (Chicago: Henry Regnery Co., 3rd revised ed., 1966); 705–710; on the socialist calculation debate, see, Trygve J. B. Hoff, *Economic Calculation in the Socialist Society* [1949] (Indianapolis: Liberty Press, 1981); Don Lavoie, ed., "An Economic Critique of Socialism," *The Journal of Libertarian Studies,* vol. 5, no. 1 (Winter, 1981); Don Lavoie, *Rivalry and Central Planning: The Socialist Calculation Debate Reconsidered* (New York: Cambridge University Press, 1985); and David Ramsey Steele, *From Marx to Mises: Post-Capitalist Society and the Challenge of Economic Calculation* (La Salle, Illinois: Open Court, 1992).

[9]See, Vera Lutz, *Central Planning for the Market Economy* (London: Longmans, Green & Co., Ltd., 1969); John Jewkes, *The New Ordeal by Planning* (New York: St. Martin's Press, 1968).

[10]See introduction to *The Global Failure of Socialism* ed. Richard M. Ebeling (Hillsdale: Hillsdale College Press, 1992), 2–3; and Richard M. Ebeling, "Austrian Economics and the Decline of Socialism Around the World," *Journal of Private Enterprise,* vol. 5, no. 1 (Fall, 1989), 129–136; also, Peter J. Boettke, *Why Perestroika Failed: The Politics and Economics of Socialist Transformation* (London/New York: Rutledge, 1993), 21–25.

[11] See the articles on the Yugoslavian experiment in, Eirik Furubotn and Svetozar Pejovich, ed., *The Economics of Property Rights* (Cambridge, Mass.: Ballinger Publishing Co., 1974), 227–276; and, David L. Prychitko, *Marxism and Workers' Self-Management* (New York: Greenwood Press, 1991).

[12] See, Friederich A. Hayek, "The Results of Human Action But Not of Human Design," *Studies in Philosophy, Politics, and Economics* (Chicago: University of Chicago Press, 1967), 96–105.

[13] Sudha Shenoy, "Some Implications of the Hayekian (and Austrian) Analysis for Eastern Europe," an appendix to Friedrich A. Hayek, *Order—With or Without Design?* (London: The Centre for Research into Communist Economies, 1989), 190 & 193.

[14] Walter Eucken, *The Foundations of Economics: History and Theory in the Analysis of Economic Reality* (Chicago: University of Chicago Press, 1951), 134.

[15] See, Guenter Reimann, *The Black Market: Inevitable Child of Statism* (Hinsdale, Ill.: Henry Regnery Co., 1948), 13–19.

[16] The next several paragraphs draw upon a recent paper of mine, Richard M. Ebeling, "Economic Reform in Russia: The First Year's Failures and This Year's Prospects," *News and Views*, vol. 1, no. 2 (Waleska, Ga.: Center for Entrepreneurship and Free Enterprise at Reinhardt College, Spring, 1993).

[17] For examples of black market activity in the Soviet Union, particularly during the Brezhnev era, see, Hedrick Smith, *The Russians* (New York: Quadrangle Books, 1976); Robert G. Kaiser, *Russia: The People and the Power* (New York; Atheneum, 1976); David K. Shipler, *Russia: Broken Idols, Solemn Dreams* (New York: Times Books, 1983); and Michael Binyon, *Life in Russia* (New York: Pantheon Books, 1983).

[18] Lev Timofeyev, *Russia's Secret Rulers: How the Government and Criminal Mafia Exercise Their Power* (New York: Alfred A. Knopf, 1992), 57–58 & 64.

[19] Ibid.

[20] Ibid.

[21] Konstantin Simis, *U.S.S.R. The Corrupt Society: The Secret World of Soviet Capitalism* (New York: Simon and Schuster, 1982), 235.

[22] David Remnick, *Lenin's Tomb: The Last Days of the Soviet Empire* (New York: Random House, 1993), 184.

[23] Vitaly A. Naishul, *The Supreme and Last Stage of Socialism* (London: The Centre for Research into Communist Economies, 1991); on the nature and structure of this system of privilege and power, see, Michael Voslensky, *Nomenklatura, The Soviet Ruling Class: An Insider's Report* (New York: Doubleday & Co., 1984) and Mervyn Matthews, *Privilege in the*

Soviet Union: A Study of Elite Life-Styles under Communism (London: George Allen & Unwin, 1978).

[24]Hedrick Smith, *The Russians,* 228–230; Robert Kaiser, *Russia: The People and the Power,* 324–326.

[25]Jan Winiecki, *Resistance to Change in the Soviet Economic System: A Property Rights Approach* (New York: Routledge, 1991).

[26]The economics literature has come to call the pursuit of political profits, "rent-seeking" or "directly-unproductive profit-seeking." See, James M. Buchanan, Robert D. Tollison and Gordon Tullock, eds., *Toward a Theory of the Rent-Seeking Society* (College Station: Texas A&M University Press, 1980); and David C. Colander, ed., *Neoclassical Political Economy: The Analysis of Rent-Seeking and DUP Activities* (Cambridge, Mass.: Ballinger Publishing Co., 1984).

[27]Janos Kornai, *The Socialist System: The Political Economy of Communism* (Princeton: Princeton University Press, 1992), 140–145.

[28]"Yeltsin Offers Everyone Privatization Checks: The President of Russia's Address to his Fellow Citizens," *Izvestia,* August 20, 1992 in *The Current Digest of the Post-Soviet Press* (Sept. 16, 1992), 1–4.

[29]"Three Basic Options for Privatization," *Izvestia* , Sept. 28, 1992 in *The Current Digest of the Post-Soviet Press* (Nov. 4, 1992), 7–8; Bozidar Djelic, "Mass Privatization in Russia: The Role of Vouchers," *RFE/RL Research Report* (Oct. 16, 1992), 43; Keith Bush, "Industrial Privatization in Russia: A Progress Report," *RFE/RL Research Report* (Feb. 12, 1993), 32–34.

[30]Tatyana Boikova, "Gavrill Popov—I Refuse to Play Cards," *Megapolis-Express,* July 8, 1992 in *The Current Digest of the Post-Soviet Press* (Aug. 5, 1992), 29.

[31]Vasily Selyunin, "The Third Attempt—Postponing the Restoration of Private Ownership 'Until Better Times' Means Postponing Forever," *Izvestia,* September 22, 1992 in *The Current Digest of the Post-Soviet Press* (Oct. 28, 1992), 15–16.

[32]Interview with Larisa Piyasheva, "Vouchers Won't Bring Greater Freedom," *Pravda,* Sept. 5, 1992 in *The Current Digest of the Post-Soviet Press* (Oct. 7, 1992), 30.

[33]Igor Karpenko, "The Privatization Program for 1993," *Izvestia,* May 20, 1993 in *The Current Digest of the Post-Soviet Press* (June 23, 1993), 6–7.

[34]Interview with Larisa Piyasheva, "Chubais Wanted to Call Me a Bolshevik," *Smena,* June 2, 1993 in *The Current Digest of the Post-Soviet Press* (July, 21, 1993), 16.

[35]Jonas Bernstein, "A Land of Individualists," *The American Spectator* (June, 1993), 49.

[36]Igor Baranovsky, "A Bomb for a Businessman"; and Vladimir Ionov, "Everybody Protects Himself to the Best of His Intellect," *Moscow News*, no. 21 (May 21, 1993), 7.

[37]For examples of the problems of doing business in Russia during the last years of the Soviet Union and in the first years of the new Russia, see, Roger Boyes, *The Hard Road to Market: Gorbachev, the Underworld and the Rebirth of Capitalism* (London: Secker & Warburg, 1990); A. Craig Copetas, *Bear Hunting with the Politburo: A Gritty First-Hand Account of Russia's Young Entrepreneurs—and Why Soviet-Style Capitalism Can't Work* (New York: Simon & Schuster, 1991); Stanislav Tverdohlebov and Thomas P. Mullen, *Russia and Its Mysterious Market: Getting Started and Doing Business in the New Russian Marketplace* (Closter, N.J.: Tradewinds Press, 1992); and Bill Thomas and Charles Sutherland, *Red Tape: Adventure Capitalism in the New Russia* (New York: Dutton, 1992).

[38]Valery Kornev, "A Young Entrepreneur Becomes the First President of Kalmykia," *Izvestia* (April 13, 1993) in *The Current Digest of the Post-Soviet Press* (May, 12, 1993), 1.

[39]A. Yevtushenko, "Local Elections on the Eve of a Decisive Battle," *Komsomolskaya Pravda* (April 13, 1993) in *The Current Digest of the Post-Soviet Press* (May 12, 1993), 2.

[40]Vladimir Ladny, "The Man Who Bought a Republic," *Komsomolskaya Pravda* (April 30, 1993) in *The Current Digest of the Post-Soviet Press* (May, 26, 1993), 22.

[41]Boris Fyodorov, "Russia's Financial Policy After the Referendum," *Izvestia* (May 8, 1993) in *The Current Digest of the Post-Soviet Press* (June 9, 1993), 8–9.

[42]On the problem of inflation in the post-Soviet era in Russia, see Richard M. Ebeling, "Economic Reform in Russia."

[43]Nelly Bul-Zidgenidze and Len Karpinsky, "Meeting the World... Meeting Colleagues," *Moscow News*, no. 9 (February 25, 1993), 8.

[44]For a brief discussion of some of the political and economic trends among intellectuals and economists in the West in the wake of the fall of communism, see, Richard M. Ebeling, "Liberalism and Collectivism in the 20th Century," *Political Studies* (1993).

[45]Otto Latsis, "Roundtable Participants Seek to Plant Fear of Civil War and Promise to Combine the Uncombinable," *Izvestia* (April 8, 1993) in *The Current Digest of the Post-Soviet Press* (May 5, 1993), 32.

[46]Ibid.

[47]Boris Yeltsin, "The Policy of Reforms is Now Under the People's Protection," *Rossiiskiye vesti* (April 30, 1993) in *The Current Digest of the Post-Soviet Press* (May 26, 1993), 7–8.

[48]Victor Chernomyrdin, "The Processes of Reforming Our Economy Have, By and Large, Become Irreversible," *Rossiiskiye vesti* (April 30, 1993) in *The Current Digest of the Post-Soviet Press* (May 26, 1993), 7–8.

[49]Ibid.

[50]Mikhail Berger, "The Ministry of Economics Aspires to the Role of the State Planning Committee," *Izvestia* (May 5, 1993) in *The Current Digest of the Post-Soviet Press* (June 2, 1993), 8–9; and Irina Savvateyeva, "A 'Lobnoye Mesto' for Reforms?—That's What the Ministry of Economics Could Become Under Oleg Lobov," *Komsomolskaya Pravda* (May 14, 1993) in *The Current Digest of the Post-Soviet Press* (June 9, 1993), 6.

[51]Sergei Glazyev, "On Industrial Policy in Russia," *Rossiiskiye Vesti* (April 21, 1993) in *The Current Digest of the Post-Soviet Press* (June 2, 1993), 11–12; and Aleksandr Bekker, "The Government Is Putting Everything on the Altar of the Fatherland—The Evolution of Minister Sergei Glazyev," *Sevodnya* (May 12, 1993) in *The Current Digest of the Post-Soviet Press* (June 9, 1993), 7.

[52]Cf., the insightful remarks by Yves Guyot, *The Tyranny of Socialism* (New York: Charles Scribner's Sons, 1894), xxxvii and xl.

[53]Cf., Oskar Morgenstern, *The Limits of Economics* (London: William Hodge and Co., Ltd., 1937).

[54]Irina Hakamada, "Business and Power: Dialogue Without an Outcome," *Moscow News,* No. 23 (June 4, 1993), 11.

[55] Robert Flint, *Socialism* (London: Sir Isaac Pitman & Sons, Ltd., 1908), 164.

[56] Paul Leroy-Beaulieu, *Collectivism* (London: John Murray, 1908), 205–206.

[57]On the reemergence of civil society and alternative social and political structures, especially during the last ten years in the former Soviet Union, see, Geoffrey A. Hosking, *The Awakening of the Soviet Union* (Cambridge: Harvard University Press, 1990); and Geoffrey A. Hosking, Jonathan Aves Peter, J. S. Duncan, eds., *The Road to Post-Communism: Independent Political Movements in the Soviet Union, 1985-1991* (London: Pinter Publishers, 1992); and in Eastern Europe, Vladimir Tismaneanu, *Reinventing Politics: Eastern Europe from Stalin to Havel* (New York: The Free Press, 1992).

[58]Stephen Seplow, "Change Comes Slowly to Russia's Farmbelt," *Knight-Ridder/Tribune Business News* (June 14, 1993).

[59]Yury Karpenko, "Grounds for Optimism," *Izvestia* (May 15, 1993) in *The Current Digest of the Post-Soviet Press* (June 16, 1993), 27.

[60]Cf. for example, the arguments made along these lines by Robert V. Daniels, *The End of the Communist Revolution* (London/New York: Routledge, 1993), 181–183.

[61]See, Richard M. Ebeling, "The Legacy of Soviet Socialism: Broken Souls and Self-Doubt," particularly the postscript on "The Failed Coup and the Rebirth of a Free Russia," in *The Global Failure of Socialism*, ed. Richard M. Ebeling (Hillsdale: Hillsdale College Press, 1992), 153–170.

[62]See, Serge Schmemann, "On Both Sides: Disarray and Indecision," *New York Times* (Oct. 7, 1993), A8; and Fred Hiatt, Margaret Shapiro, and Lee Hockstader, "The Night Yeltsin Teetered: Russia's Fate Was Decided Largely by Chance," *Washington Post* (Oct. 8, 1993), A1 & A32.

[63]"Yeltsin Dissolves Parliament, Calls New Elections," *The Current Digest of the Post-Soviet Press* (Oct. 20, 1993), 1–19; "Moscow Standoff: Regions, Centrists Push Demands," *The Current Digest of the Post-Soviet Press* (Oct. 27, 1993), 1–16 & 20; "Yeltsin Foes Force Showdown, Are Crushed," *The Current Digest of the Post-Soviet Press* (Nov. 3, 1933), 1–25.

[64]"Scanning the Aftermath: A Wide Range of Views," *The Current Digest of the Post-Soviet Press* (Nov. 10, 1993), 1–13 & 32.

[65]David Remnick, "Letter from Moscow: The Hangover," *The New Yorker* (Nov. 22, 1993), 51–65; Semyon Reznik, "The Real Choices in Russia Are Few," *Washington Times* (Dec. 7, 1993), A17; and James P. Gallagher and Howard Witt, "Russia Vote No Model for Democracy," *Chigaco Tribune,* Perspectives Section (Dec. 12, 1993), 1 & 4.

[66]"Yeltsin Wants to Serve Out Term," *RFE/RL Daily Report* (Nov. 8, 1993), 1; and Celestine Bohlen, "Yeltsin Backs Away from Early Presidential Election," *New York Times* (Nov. 7, 1993), A3.

[67]"Yeltsin Denies Having Canceled Early Presidential Elections," *RFE/ RL Daily Report* (Nov. 16, 1993), 1.

[68]"Yeltsin Can Serve Out His Full Term, Election Chief Says," *UPI* (Dec. 14, 1993).

[69]"Yeltsin Decrees That Federation Council Is to Be Elected," and "Yeltsin Changes State Duma's Structure, Election Procedures," *The Current Digest of the Post-Soviet Press* (Nov. 10, 1993), 16–18.

[70]Daniel Sneider, "Yeltsin's New Deal Reneges on Promises to Republics," *The Christian Science Monitor* (Nov. 5, 1993), 1 & 4; "Yeltsin Constitution Ditches Republic Sovereignty," and "Who's Really Drafting Constitution, Election Law?" *The Current Digest of the Post-Soviet Press* (Nov. 24, 1993), 6–9; also, Vasily Kononenko, "The Constitutional Conference Approves the Draft of a New Constitution for Russia," *Izvestia* (July 13, 1993) in *The Current Digest of the Post-Soviet Press* (August 11, 1993), 1–2.

[71]Julia Wishnevsky, "The Role of the Media in the Parliamentary Election Campaign," *RFE/RL Research Report* (Nov.19, 1993), 8–12; Jamey Gambrell, "Moscow: Storm over the Press," *New York Review of Books* (Dec. 16, 1993), 69–74; Celestine Bohlen, "Candidates Take to Airwaves as Russian Vote Approaches," *New York Times* (Nov. 27, 1993), 1–4; Lee Hockstader, "Yeltsin Threatens to Yank TV Time from Opponents," *Washington Post* (Nov. 27, 1993); Wendy Sloane, "Roll the Cameras—Russia's Politicians Are on the Air," *Christian Science Monitor* (Dec. 2, 1993); Serge Schmemann, "Russian Election Coverage Ranges from Partisan to Sophisticated," *New York Times* (Dec. 5, 1993); Yelena Yakovleva, "Which Newspapers and Magazines in Russia Receive Subsidies and Why," *Izvestia* (Aug. 26, 1993) in *The Current Digest of the Post-Soviet Press* (Sept. 22, 1993), 27–28.

[72]"Twenty-One Parties Registered 100,000 Signatures," and "Blocs Entitled to Participate in Elections," *RFE/RL Daily Report* (Nov. 8, 1993), 2; "Thirteen Parties to Participate in Elections," and "Parties Participating in Elections," *RFE/RL Daily Report* (Nov. 11, 1993), 1; "The First Stage of Election Campaign Is Over," *Moscow News,* no. 46 (Nov. 12, 1993), 1.

[73]Olga Bychkova and Viktor Alexeyenko, "Electoral Blocs Awaiting Judgment of Voters," *Moscow News,* no. 44 (Oct. 29, 1993), 3; also, Justin Burke, "Rift Grows Among Russian Democrats," *Christian Science Monitor* (Oct. 21, 1993), 1 & 4; and Justin Burke and Wendy Sloane, "Having Crushed Rebellion, Yeltsin Government Turns Against Itself," *Christian Science Monitor* (Oct. 29, 1993), 1 & 4; Lee Hockstader, "Russians Hit Middle of the Road: Reformers, Hard-Liners Starting to Look Alike as Election Nears," *Washington Post* (Nov. 30, 1993), A19 & A22; and, Daniel Sneider, "The Russian Vote: A Profusion of Parties Competes for New Parliament," *Christian Science Monitor* (Dec. 8, 1993), 6–7.

[74]Howard Witt, "Feet Up, Yeltsin Allies Rest While Rivals Campaign," *Chicago Tribune* (Dec. 9, 1993), 1 & 6; Serge Schmemann, "Yeltsin Campaigns for Yeltsin and Not for Mere Politicians," *New York Times* (Dec. 10, 1993), A1 & A9.

[75]Jonas Bernstein, "Politics Unique in Arty St. Petersburg," *Washington Times* (Nov. 28, 1993), A1 & A11; Daniel Sneider, "Russian Politicians Stump with Nationalist Rhetoric," *Christian Science Monitor* (Nov. 29, 1993), 1 & 18; Justin Burke, "Personalities, Not Laws, Rule in New Russia," *Christian Science Monitor* (Nov. 29, 1993), 4; Wendy Sloane, "Russia's Agrarian Party Runs Against Land Reform," *Christian Science Monitor* (Dec. 1, 1993), 4; Fred Hiatt, "Moscow Voters Barely Notice Election Campaign," *Washington Post* (Dec. 3, 1993); Serge Schme-

mann, "Russia Election: Some Rah-Rah, No Sis-Boom-Bah," *New York Times* (Dec. 3, 1993), A3; Fred Hiatt, "Candidate Finds More Reform a Hard Sell in Russia," *Washington Post* (Dec. 4, 1993), A23; Celestine Bohlen, "Russian Nationalist Adds Pitch for Women's Vote to a Flamboyant Campaign," *New York Times* (Dec. 7, 1993); Daniel Sneider, "Russian Communists See Propsects Improve in Campaign Stretch," *Christian Science Monitor* (Dec. 7, 1993), 3; Serge Schmemann, "Vote? Anger Pierces Russia's Suffering Heartland," *New York Times* (Dec. 8, 1993), A3; James P. Gallagher, "Yeltsin Foes Put on New Face for Election," *Chicago Tribune* (Dec. 10, 1993); Lee Hockstader, "Economy—and Yeltsin—Sag in Russia's Rust Belt," *Washington Post* (Dec. 10, 1993), A1 & A51; Howard Witt and James P. Gallagher, "Russian Vote: Anxious Step into the Unknown," *Chicago Tribune* (Dec. 12, 1993), 1 & 20.

[76]"Final Public Opinion Data Published," *RFE/RL Daily Report* (Dec. 3, 1993), 1

[77]Howard Witt and James P. Gallagher, "Russian Vote: Anxious Step into the Unknown," *Chicago Tribune* (Dec. 12, 1993), 1 & 20.

[78]"Latest Unofficial Preliminary Results," *RFE/RL Daily Report* (Dec. 14, 1993), 1; Adi Ignatius, "Yeltsin's Foes Outnumber Allies in Duma," *Wall Street Journal* (Dec. 14, 1993), A10.

[79]On Vladimir Zhirinovsky's background and views, see, John B. Dunlop, *The Rise of Russia and the Fall of the Soviet Empire* (Princeton: Princeton University Press, 1993), 154–158; David Remnick, *Lenin's Tomb: The Last Days of the Soviet Empire* (New York: Random House, 1993), 524–525; and Serge Schmemann, "Moscovite with Bravado: Vladimir Volfovich Zhirinovsky," *New York Times* (Dec. 14, 1993), A1 & A6.

[80]"Russia's Choice Recoups in Single-Member Districts," *RFE/RL Daily Report* (Dec. 16, 1993), 1.

[81]Vladimir Gurevich, "Quiet! Restoration Is under Way," *Moscow News* (June 20, 1993) in *The Current Digest of the Post-Soviet Press* (July 14, 1993), 26–27; Mikhail Berger, "Ministry of Economics Is Preparing an 'Indicative Five-Year Plan' for Us," *Izvestia* (June 29, 1993) in *The Current Digest of the Post-Soviet Press* (July 28, 1993), 24; "Yeltsin, Shmelyov Give Prescriptions for Economy," in *The Current Digest of the Post-Soviet Press* (Aug. 11, 1993), 18–20; "Lobov's 'Anti-Reform' Plan Stalled (For Now)" in *The Current Digest of the Post-Soviet Press* (Sept. 1, 1993), 1–5; "The Battle over Economic Policy Goes on," in *The Current Digest of the Post-Soviet Press* (Sept. 8, 1993), 1–6; Aleksandr Bekker, "Boris Fyodorov: 'The Next Two Weeks Will be a Time of Political Choice,'" *Sevodnya* (Aug. 24, 1993) in *The Current Digest of the Post-Soviet Press* (Sept. 22, 1993), 11–13; Mikhail Leontyev, "Boris

Fyodorov: The Government on the Eve of a Decisive Choice Between Financial Catastrophe and Stabilization," *Sevodnya* (Sept. 3, 1993) and Igor Petrov, "Medicine Is Never Sweet—The Ministry of Finance Is Preparing a Stabilization Program," *Rossiiskiye vesti* (September 3, 1993) in *The Current Digest of the Post-Soviet Press* (Sept. 29, 1993), 8–10; "Counterreformers Launch Yet Another Drive," in *The Current Digest of the Post-Soviet Press* (Oct. 6, 1993), 8–10; "Gaidar Back, Lobov Out: Analyzing the Politcs," and "Political Solution Is the Key, Says Gaidar," in *The Current Digest of the Post-Soviet Press* (October 13, 1993), 1–9; "Economic Populism: A Look into the Abyss," *The Current Digest of the Post-Soviet Press* (October 20, 1993), 20–21.

[82]Serge Schemann, "Yeltsin Approves New Constitution Widening His Role," *New York Times* (Nov. 9, 1993), A1 & A6; Celestine Bohlen, "Yeltsin Opens Campaign for the Charter," *New York Times* (Nov. 10, 1993), A6.

[83]"The Text of the Draft Constitution," *The Current Digest of the Post-Soviet Press* (December 8, 1993), 4–16, especially 6–7.

[84]See, Richard M. Ebeling, "The Political Economy of Privatization and Market Reform in Russia," *World Capitalism Review* (Oct. 1993), 18–22.

[85]Richard W. Stevenson, "Vouchers Become Hot Tickets for Russian Bulls," *New York Times* (Nov. 10, 1993), C1 & C6.

[86]"Momentum of Privatization Undaunted by Power Struggle," *Commersant: The Russian Business Weekly* (Sept. 29, 1993), 29–31.

[87]Lee Hockstader, "Russian Vote Seen as Key to Reforms," *Washington Post* (Nov. 17, 1993), A32; and Steven Erlanger, "Russia Showing Gains in Economic Performance," *New York Times* (Dec. 4, 1993), 1 & 4.

[88]"Decree of the President of the Russian Federation: On the Regulation of Land Relations and the Development of Agrarian Reform in Russia," *Izvestia* (Oct. 29, 1993) in *The Current Digest of the Post-Soviet Press* (Nov. 24, 1993), 14–16; Elisabeth Rubinfien, "Russia Moves to Dismantle Collective-Farming System," *Wall Street Journal* (Oct. 27, 1993), A18; Olga Berezhnaya, "Private Ownership of Agricultural Land Has Been Legalized," *Moscow News* no. 46 (Nov. 12, 1993), 7; and, Don Van Atta, "Yeltsin Decree Finally Ends 'Second Serfdom' in Russia," *RFE/RL Research Report* (Nov. 19, 1993), 33–39.

[89]Andrei Sizov, "Will the Land Market Work?" *Moscow News* no. 45 (Nov. 5, 1993), 1–2; Semyon Reznik, "Yeltsin's Risky Land Reform," *Washington Times* (Nov. 8, 1993); and "Land Reform: How Much Reform Does It Entail?" *The Current Digest of the Post-Soviet Press* (Dec. 1, 1993), 8–11.

[90]Yelena Martynova, "Aleksandr Kotonkov: We Discovered a State Within the State," *Megapolis-Express* (Aug. 25, 1993) in *The Current Digest of the Post-Soviet Press* (Sept. 15, 1993), 7.

[91]See, Bill Thomas and Charles Sutherland, *Red Tape: Adventure Capitalism in the New Russia* (New York: Dutton Books, 1992), 25–40.

[92]See, Richard M. Ebeling, "Some Warnings for the East: What Socialist Countries Need to Know," *Freedom Daily* (November 1992), 6–10.

[93]Richard M. Ebeling, "Democratized Privilege: The New Mercantilism," *Freedom Daily* (February 1991), 6–10; and Ebeling, "Producer Interests vs. the Public Interest: The Origin of Democratized Privilege," *Freedom Daily* (March 1991), 6–10.

[94]"Reforming Russia's Economy: Cruel to be Kind," *The Economist* (Dec. 11, 1993), 23–25.

Aleksandas Shtromas

The Transition to a Free Market System: The Hillsdale Plan and the Other Plans

I. Post-Communist Societies: Achievements and Problems

The anti-communist revolutions in the U.S.S.R. and Eastern and Central Europe, having started in 1989, were triumphantly concluded on August 21, 1991, with the collapse of communist rule in the Soviet Union and with the Soviet Union itself being formally dissolved in December of the same year. The fall of communism in the U.S.S.R. and the subsequent dissolution of the Soviet state made the victory of the anti-communist revolutions in Eastern and Central Europe, the Baltic States, Moldova, the Transcaucasian nations and Russia itself secure and irreversible. The world has not only entered into the post-communist but the post-ideological era.

Post-communism virtually brought to conclusion the 20th century which, unleashed in 1914 by World War I, became the age of ideology—the age of active search for panaceas against the terrible ills of mankind (ills that have made possible the unprecedented tragedy of the war) in globally conceived universal ideologies such as communism and fascism; it was, accordingly, also the age of defense and struggle against aggressive undertakings of the various communist and fascist ideological regimes and of resistance to totalitarian temptations these ideologies quite forcefully propelled around the world. If the end of World War II in 1945 saw the disappearance of the fascist ideological challenge from the world's stage, the failure of the communist-restorationist putsch in Moscow in August, 1991 did the same to Marxist communism—to that ideological challenge which was the first to appear and the last to crumble. Into the next millennium the formerly communist ruled lands and their captive nations enter as genuinely free peoples engaged in an intense and freewheeling search for their organic cultural, social, and political identities as well as for their fairly defined places in the world, alongside, and in proper association with, other free nations. That the nations of the former Soviet domain have become really free is eloquently proved by the fact that, having been liberated from communist oppression, they promptly affirmed themselves as truly independent political entities and in no time successfully established themselves as fully sovereign and separate nation-states.

Political freedom is, however, not an unmitigated blessing. For it also implies the free nation's liberty to engage in conflict with other nations when the latter either deny it sovereign rights or contest its possession or claim of a territory which that nation considers legitimately belonging to it. Fortunately, there were no such conflicts involving Russia, which, to many people's surprise, quite willingly conceded its predominance over other nations of the former Soviet domain. But the Armenian-Azerbaijani dispute over Nagorno-Karabakh, the Georgian denial of sovereignty to Abkhazia and South Ossetia, and the rebellion of the Russian-speaking part of the population of Moldova's Transistria against Moldovan sovereignty over that region have created very acute and sometimes bloody conflicts which to this day remain unresolved and continue unabated. Sad as they may be, such conflicts are one of the clearest demonstrations of the respective peoples' genuine political liberty. It is only under the conditions of liberty that people may freely choose to engage in resolute struggle for what they believe are their vital interests and inalienable rights. And the more political liberty the 21st century sees, the more conflicts of this kind will probably proliferate. This is the natural and therefore unavoidable illness of growth and maturation of all social organisms, e.g., of nations.

The acquisition of political freedom by the post-communist nations was also clearly expressed by their immediate transition from submissive meekness to suddenly uninhibited practice of freedom of speech; freedom of press; freedom of public manifestations; freedom of organizing various political parties and other public bodies; freedom of religion; freedom of movement within the country, of travelling abroad and of returning home; as well as of other basic freedoms and human rights which were absolutely denied them under communist rule. Due to their unrestrained realization of all these newly acquired freedoms, the post-communist nations have developed pluralistic political systems which have provided them the opportunity of holding free and genuinely competitive democratic elections which most (though not yet all) of them have already taken advantage of more than once. This is to say that in the post-communist lands the foundations of a liberal-democratic political order have been already quite firmly established, too. When, for example, in Georgia the democratically elected president Zviad Gamsakhurdia tried to abolish political pluralism by establishing a semi-fascist one-party dictatorship, opposition forces initially suppressed by him somehow managed to come together and launch a successful counter-attack. They ousted Gamsakhurdia from power, forcefully reasserted political pluralism, and resolutely restored in Georgia the fledgling foundations of a liberal-democratic political order.

Political freedom and the pluralistic, liberal democratic

order, as the natural outgrowth of that freedom, were, however, proved to be, though absolutely necessary, insufficient prerequisites for assuring the transition from a totalitarian to a free social system in any of the post-communist lands. Although the democratically established post-communist governments of those lands have genuinely set themselves the task of privatizing the economy, instituting the free market and fostering all other institutions necessary for the recreation of a civil society functioning under the rule of law, none has so far succeeded in substantially advancing, let alone fulfilling, that task.

The most easily observable and more or less clearly definable explanation of this peculiar impasse is institutional. Indeed, the democratically formed and radical reform oriented post-communist governments inherited and swallowed hook, line, and sinker the monstrous state apparatuses of the old communist regimes that continue to function as if nothing has changed and that not only strongly resist all attempts by the new governments to reform, reduce, and substantially change their structural-functional identity but are also sabotaging the respective governments' efforts to use them as instruments of reforms aimed at creating the new free social and economic systems, or—which is one and the same thing—their efforts to transform the present social and economic systems into authentic civil societies.

Indeed, the post-communist governments wrongly assumed that the collapse of Communist Party rule and their own ascendancy to supreme political authority marked the end of the victorious anti-totalitarian revolution while in fact it was just its very beginning. Instead of, in the first place, destroying the old state apparatuses and liberating social and economic processes from the restrictive confines the apparatuses of totalitarian rule impose upon these processes, they started presiding over these same apparatuses and some, out of dogmatic respect for the principles of the rule of law, even engaged in playing the game of law abiding continuity with the old Soviet-type order. By so doing they have practically shot themselves in the foot.

In a very communist tradition, these new anti-communist governments have entirely disregarded the fact that political forms and processes are inseparable from their substance and have wrongly assumed therefore that the political institutions they have inherited from the past will serve them as pliantly and obediently as they used to serve the Communist Party. And they probably would have done so, if the new governments were content to keep intact, preside over, and further strengthen the totalitarian system which the old communist state machinery so aptly embodied. But the new governments, by poising themselves to dismantle that system, have alienated the entrenched state apparatuses which successfully sabotaged the governments' more radical moves and thus managed not only to insure self-preservation but, through the state bureaucracies' envoys in the representative councils, also to force the governments, ostensibly for the sake of social cohesion and people's welfare, to proceed with the reforms in a slow, halfhearted manner and under their—the state bureaucracies'—total supervision and control. This is how the reformist post-communist governments, by having put themselves into the position of the authority presiding over the conservative Soviet-type state apparatuses, have become prisoners of these apparatuses which have virtually incapacitated them and stalled the reform processes initiated by them. It is exactly because of this that the projected reforms of the respective social-economic systems amounted to what the continental criminal lawyers call "attempts with faulty means"—not only did such irresolute, internally contradictory reforms fail to yield any substantial positive results but, as all half measures inevitably do, they significantly worsened the overall social and economic situation. Ironically, economically and in many other related respects of social life, this situation became even

worse than it had been under superficially orderly and predictable "mature socialism."

II. The "Other Plans" of Transition to the Free Market

This most obvious institutional explanation of the present
crisis in post-communist lands does not tell, however, the
whole story. The reformist governments themselves, in addition to their conservative opponents in the state machinery and in the representative bodies inherited by those governments from the communist past, must be held responsible to a great degree for failing to insure a radical dismantling of the communist-totalitarian legacy. The policies of
reforms freely chosen by those governments were in themselves so irresolute and inconsistent that, even if fulfilled
without any substantial hindrance on the part of their powerful opponents, they would hardly be able to bring about
the desired transition to a free civil society functioning under modern liberal law.

Again, one could offer many explanations for the post-
communist governments' failure to elaborate policies of
transition which would be adequate to the task they have set
themselves to accomplish. Fear of massive bankruptcies and
of ensuing mass unemployment which, presumably, would
have followed a drastic transition to a free market system
drained their courage to go straight for the introduction of
such a system. The instinctive distrust of people (who, as the
new rulers see it, being spoiled and demoralized by their
socialist upbringing and experience, would hardly be able
to work productively in a free enterprise environment, stealing instead everything put in that environment at their disposal and thus altogether destroying whatever has remained
of the countries' productive facilities), pushed them not
merely towards maintaining but even strengthening the
state's supervision and control over the slowly but massively

evolving (though mainly evolving beyond the pale of the still valid socialist laws) private economic activities.

For the same reasons, and in order to avoid trouble by too drastically injuring too many vested interests entrenched in the old statist economic system, their plans for privatization leave most enterprises in the state's hands for practically an indefinite period of time and also make sure that the state is firmly in charge of the privatization process itself. And this usually tends to insure the status quo or, in other words, that the enterprises, even after privatization, basically remain in the hands of the same people who were in charge of them yesterday and remain so today.[1]

In Hungary the privatization of large state industries until July 30, 1993, when the government at last declared that mass privatization would start in early 1994, was not even in the government's plans. Instead, Hungary was speedily promoting new economic ventures based on attracting large sums of foreign investment. In this way the post-communist government was trying to build a new modern economy almost from scratch. It reckoned that with the development of this new economy, the old state industrial enterprises would either adjust and get incorporated into it or, of course the government permitting, they would be allowed to die their natural deaths. Apparently these expectations did not materialize and, as one sees from its July 30th Declaration, the Hungarian government was forced to have a change of heart on that issue and start seriously contemplating a special privatization program for its state industry.

In Poland all industrial state enterprises have been transformed into joint-stock companies. The stock, however, belongs to the state and is held by the Ministry for Privatization, which alone has the right to decide what enterprises are ready to be put on sale to private bidders, and then either sells the shares of these enterprises directly to such bidders or releases them onto the embryonic stock market. It is not surprising, therefore, that by 1993 over 80 percent of Poland's state enterprises were still in the state's full ownership, producing mainly loss and loot. In most of the remaining 20 percent the state still maintains a strong, sometimes even a controlling presence. The latest Polish government led by Hanna Suchocka has tried to speed up the process of privatization but her privatization bill was defeated in the Sejm (Parliament) as too radical and has had to be substantially revised and reduced. Nevertheless, the passage of this watered-down bill has been met by massive workers strikes which for the time being have thwarted implementation. But even when these temporary obstacles are eventually removed and the government's privatization bill is finally realized, its implementation will put on the market only a relatively small proportion of Polish state enterprises. The bulk of Polish heavy industry will still remain the undivided property of the state, and no one can tell how long this situation will last.

In former Czechoslovakia privatization has been divided into two separate processes: one for small enterprises ("small privatization") and another for large enterprises ("large privatization"). Small privatization is underway in Czechoslovakia, spreading quickly and on the whole successfully. For the large enterprises the process is, however, sluggish. The Czechs have invented the voucher system of privatization, whereby citizens can acquire shares of privatized enterprises in exchange for vouchers issued to each of them on equal terms by the government for a nominal fee. The distributionary sales of vouchers lasted until the spring of 1993 and on May 24, 1993, for the first time, shares in about one thousand companies released for privatization in 1992 were made available to the public in exchange for their vouchers. The process of privatization which has thus just started promises to be quite protracted—according to the government's plans, it should last for at least five years, but it may last much longer if, for example, there are not enough bidders for buying the shares of certain enterprises.

It goes without saying that before the enterprises are sold, they remain state property; and the state is in charge of selling them, too. This means that unprofitable enterprises are destined to remain in the state's domain forever, unless the state deliberately chooses to kill them off by stopping their subsidies and declaring them bankrupt, very much like it was planned until recently in Hungary.

This rather moderate privatization plan elaborated by Czech leaders seemed to their Slovak counterparts so unbearably radical that it became one of the reasons for the subsequent split of Czechoslovakia. But, whatever the differences between the respective politicians on that score may have been, it is clear that in both the Czech Republic and Slovakia the large industrial enterprises will yet for a long time (and some, perhaps, even for good) remain a part of the state-run (or socialist) economy.

The privatization plan elaborated for Russia by her Deputy Prime Minister in charge of privatization, Anatoly Chubais, is supposed to be the most radical and prompt. Like the Czech plan, the Russian version also included voucher distribution among the members of the public. But, according to this plan, each enterprise released by the state for privatization, after it was converted (also by the state) into a joint stock holding company, will have to decide for itself in which way it wishes to be privatized. Officially approved were three such ways or legal modes of privatization from which enterprises have to choose one.

The first such mode consists of 25 percent of the shares being distributed free of charge to the workers of the enterprise as non-voting preference stock, another 10 percent of the shares the workers would have to buy at a 30 percent discount and yet another 5 percent of the shares would be allocated to the managers who would have to buy them for the full price of their 1991 book value. Altogether, the working collective would thus acquire 40 percent of the stock of which 15 percent will entitle their owners to participate in the enterprise's decision-making process by voting (i.e., 10 percent distributed among all employees, e.g., the managers, and 5 percent among the managers exclusively).

The second mode of privatization consists of the employees buying out up to 51 percent of the enterprise's shares (the controlling package) at the price 1.7 times higher than their 1991 book value. For the purchase of up to a half of these shares the employees could use their vouchers; for the rest they will have to pay cash. In order to adopt this mode of privatization it is required that not less than two-thirds of the workforce of the enterprise chose it in preference to the other two modes by secret ballot.

Finally, the third mode of privatization gives the employees twenty percent of the non-voting preference shares free and leaves them the option of buying another 20 percent at the price 1.7 times higher than their 1991 book value.

In all three modes the remaining shares—it is either 60 (in the first and third modes of privatization) or 49 percent (in the second mode of privatization) of the entire stock—remain the property of the state and are supposed to be sold by the state to members of the general public in closed-bid auctions. Thirty-five percent (in privatization modes one and three) and at least 29 percent (in privatization mode two) of these remaining shares have to be sold for vouchers and the rest, for cash. Whatever remains unsold is retained by the state as the residue of its original property rights.

The Russian privatization plan clearly states that not all of the country's industry is going to be privatized. Defense industries, major producers of energy and natural resources, vital construction and transportation outlets, etc.— in other words, all the notorious commanding heights of the country's economy—are being explicitly excluded from the process of privatization and are to remain, as before, the undivided property of the state.

Is such a plan really radical and prompt? Unfortunately, it is not. Instead of changing the Soviet economic system by transferring in real terms the state's industrial enterprises to private ownership, this plan simply tries to legitimize the situation in which Russia's industrial enterprises actually find themselves today. Indeed, after the liquidation of the Party apparatus and abolition of enforceable central planning, Russia's industrial enterprises already fell, in fact, under the effective control of their management, and partly also of their work force, as in present conditions the latter is exercising on the management a much stronger pressure than does or is able to do the government. The only real change this kind of privatization is supposed to introduce consists in the transfer of full responsibility for the performance and the fate of the thus privatized enterprise from the government to the enterprise's management and workforce themselves. The government, in other words, seeks to renounce in this way its hitherto almost a natural obligation to bail out an ineffective enterprise (granted, of course, it is not a part of the "commanding heights" of the economy) either by direct subsidy or by showering on it practically free credit. This, by the way, explains why the "reactionaries" in the economic bureaucracy so vehemently oppose this rather modest privatization plan and try, by hook or by crook, to sabotage its implementation—they do not want to lose control over a large slice of state property and the numerous plush jobs that go with it.

I very much doubt, however, that under this privatization plan the government will be really able to shed its "bail out obligation" to the "second class" industrial enterprises in a truly effective manner, since under all the three established modes of privatization the state is going to retain, at least for the foreseeable future (and may be even permanently), substantial proportions of stock in all the thus privatized enterprises. And as long as the state is going to remain in the position of an enterprise's substantial shareholder, the government will not be able to absolve itself from the responsibility for that enterprise's survival and relative well-being.

Hence, the fears of the economic bureaucrats may be a bit exaggerated, reflecting more their instinctive dislike of any change that could even slightly diminish their standing or curtail their influence than a real threat to the survival of a number of enterprises now resting comfortably under their leadership and control.

So much for the plan's radicalism. What about its promptness? According to the plan, the enterprises, which are to be privatized in the ways described above, have to be divided into annual sales-batches and put on sale one by one within the year's privatization assignment until all of them, year after year, are auctioned off. During how many years? The plan does not specify the exact number of years, but one can rest assured that this process is going to be quite protracted and not necessarily successful; for the process, as it is envisaged by this plan, gives no assurance whatsoever that, in the end, the state is going to lose its ownership of substantial proportions of stock in any of these thus privatized enterprises.

To sum it all up, privatization, as envisaged in Russia today, is in fact aimed not so much at creating truly private enterprises as at legitimizing the leading positions in these enterprises of their present managers acting under the pressure of their work force and financial protection of the government. Under such a privatization scheme, one could hardly expect Russia's economic system to change soon enough in any substantial way, a fact of which the reform-minded Russian leaders were apparently very well aware themselves, because soon after their privatization plan was adopted they started looking for certain shortcuts in the transition to the free market, besides the privatization process.

In trying to introduce the market system prior to, and independently of, privatization and, at the same time, to stabilize the ruble, Russia's then acting Prime Minister Yegor Gaidar decided to go for such a shortcut by decreeing that, effective January 1, 1992, a sudden "liberalization" of prices. The opposition, skillfully masterminded by the Supreme Soviet Chairman Ruslan Khasbulatov, thwarted this plan. With the collusion of the Central Bank, then operating under the Supreme Soviet's exclusive control, the plan was soon (by the beginning of Summer) undermined by a runaway inflation, and in December of 1992 Khasbulatov engineered Gaidar's removal from office.

It seems, however, that even without the opposition's foiling of Gaidar's plan, the latter had little chance of becoming truly successful. This was so not because the plan was too bold, as the opposition and also a number of Western analysts argued, but, on the contrary, because it was not bold and consistent enough. Some prices (e.g., those for fuel and energy which inevitably reflected on prices of all manufactured goods) under this plan have not been fully "released," in the first place; and most enterprises, in order to remain afloat in the new price situation, had to continue to rely on state subsidies and artificially cheap credits. The latter logically followed from the former and both together doomed the reform to not achieving its goal before it was even put into practice. Yeltsin and Gaidar simply did not have the guts to present the people with drastic price increases on some staple consumer goods (e.g., on vodka) and were afraid of facing the social-political consequences of the inevitable reduction in the standard of living of people who were not gainfully employed in economically successful industrial, commercial, or financial enterprises, especially the numerous administrators and other political and economic bureaucrats. Nor were they ready to cope with the possibility of multiple bankruptcies and the level of unemployment which these bankruptcies could have caused. But they did not have any better ideas on how to introduce in a sufficiently swift manner a free market situation in Russia, and they therefore made a desperate move in this direction, as the Russians say, *"na avos"*—on the off chance it might still work and create the necessary momentum for propelling Russia's economy into the free market. Predictably, it did not.

All these fears and hesitations with which the reformist governments of Russia and other post-communist lands conceived their strategies for transition, the instinctive inclination of these governments to prefer a "public choice" based, compromise-seeking policy over a policy based on a consistent and unhesitant pursuit of a straight and principled line directly leading to the institution of the free market, private ownership, and other attributes of an authentic civil society, have by themselves to a large degree determined the lack of progress in overcoming socialism's legacy in all of those countries. Their governments, in my view, simply do not know what exactly their correct strategies should be like; that is, they are not yet sure how much capitalism that strategy should strive for introducing and how much of statist socialism it should aim at retaining. And even when the respective government theoretically professes a commitment to a complete break with socialism and a belief in the necessity of instituting full-scale capitalism, it usually lacks the conviction that these goals are sufficiently popular and could in a democracy justify the cost that is entailed in the means which have to be applied in order to achieve them in an effective and resolute manner. Hence, the hesitations about what precise set of policies has to be chosen and followed through in order adequately to secure the best available results for the transition in the circumstances of that particular situation and time. This is basically why the transition policies that even the most radical post-communist governments have so far chosen do not amount to anything approaching a consistent strategy but rather represent a mixed bag of accommodating compromises trying to provide "all things to all men."

Ironically, these hesitant, irresolutely well-meaning policies do not provide for smooth or caring transition at all.

On the contrary, the retention of socialist economic forms in a liberal political environment only exacerbates the destructive qualities of socialism, increases the social dysfunctions and economic imbalances inherent in socialism to truly ruinous proportions. In a way, such policies, instead of diminishing and smoothing over the pains of transition, become in themselves the cause of some of the most damaging, crisis-generating developments in post-communist societies. This, in addition to such policies generally conserving the old system, prolonging its rot and thus inadvertently creating yet more unnecessary obstacles to the very proceedings with the transition.

This irresolute ambiguity of the genuinely reformist post-communist governments is to a great extent an exact reflection of the attitudes and orientations of the regular members of post-communist societies, including their elites. In a socialist system everyone, without exception, was deprived of a recognized independent social position or standing. The regular member of a socialist society had neither private capital nor an individually determined social status. What an individual was worth, what influence he was able to exercise, entirely depended on the position he occupied in the totalitarian structure of the socialist state. It is true that a partocratic *apparatchik's* dependence for his elitist position on that particular state was absolute—in any other state he would have surely had no chance to remain a member of any elite at all—whereas a genuine professional would be able to continue to function in the same, or even in an advanced, elitist capacity under any system and in any state. Nevertheless, under socialism, even he, the genuine professional, was able to realize his potential (of course, to the extent to which such a realization was at all possible under totalitarian socialism) only by being attached to a position within the structure of that state; on his own, without that position, he, too, was a nobody.

For example, a qualified and talented engineer could be

functional only when employed in a state enterprise; without a position in that enterprise all his professional qualifications would be wasted. True, in a post-communist society, this engineer could switch to the fledgling private sector and start earning much more than he did when working for a state enterprise. But in post-communist societies the private sector is so far functioning only in the very marginal areas of the economy and on a rather small scale, which is to say that, as a rule, it would be unable to offer our engineer an activity professionally as satisfying and fulfilling as is his job in the established state enterprise. Because of that, this engineer may prefer to stay with the state enterprise, even if lured by financial incentives to switch to the private sector.

How strongly would then our engineer be interested in his state enterprise's privatization? If he could become that enterprise's owner, he would have been very strongly interested in such a transition indeed. But instead he is sure he stands no chance of ownership, and not only because he does not have the money even to start contemplating such a possibility, but mainly because there are many people around who could, like him, aspire to ownership rights, and in the competition against such people he surely does not have a specific winning edge. He still could have had a strong interest in his state enterprise's privatization if he were sure that under new ownership it would survive and flourish and that the new owners would seek out, engage, and properly appreciate his talents and expertise. But he is not at all sure about it, while he knows that with the state at least the survival and continuous functioning of the enterprise, as well as his role within it, is going to be relatively secure. Furthermore, he also knows that in the post-communist state his chances for promotion in that enterprise, as well as generally in the state sector, are much greater than they have ever been under the socialist system, where every partocratic analphabet had a built-in promotional advantage over him and where he was destined to serve under such an analphabet-boss all his life. It is now, in the era of post-communism, that for the first time he can start aspiring to become a boss himself. Hence, there is not much incentive for our engineer to strive for the prompt privatization of his enterprise. In the new, post-communist conditions he quite comfortably functions in a system based on state ownership and does not feel a particular urge to change it.

The conclusion which follows is that the governments of the post-communist lands not only do not experience any strong public pressure boldly to go ahead with radical privatization plans, but that there is a certain intuitive reluctance on the part of quite large sections of the public to accept and follow such plans. What post-communism has revealed is the complete leveling of societies which had the misfortune of going through the socialist experiment. The total state appeared to be the only institution keeping society together, providing it, for better or for worse, with a certain hierarchical structure, without which there remained nothing but entropy. One should not be, therefore, too surprised about people of various walks of life "reactionary partocrats" and "progressive technocrats" alike—instinctively sticking, even after communism's collapse, to the total state, as the only available alternative to entropy or, which is one and the same, society's death.

The society's instinctive fear of losing the total socialist state as its only organizing device no doubt weakened immensely the government's resolve to do away with it and at the same time substantially strengthened the hand of the old state apparatus in its determination to sabotage and undermine the government's reformist drive. This is perhaps what constitutes in all post-communist lands the root cause of the procrastination with, and halfheartedness of, the reforms theoretically undertaken with the view of transforming socialism into capitalism.

So, as we see, the hindrances to the institution of radical socioeconomic change in Russia and to a large extent also in other post-communist lands are situated on three levels: the level of the surviving old institutions of the total socialist state (institutional resistance and sabotage); the level of the reformers' own ideas and plans for change (lack of vision and conviction, and, hence, of decisiveness in elaborating and pursuing an adequate and consistent strategy of change); and the level of the regular socialist man (continuing dependence on his place within the structure of the total state and, for the lack of the vision of a credibly acceptable alternative to that place, an instinctive reluctance to lose it). One should stress here the direct dependence of the third level on the second one; in other words, if the reformist leaders on the second level had come to embrace a convincingly clear vision of radical change and pursued that vision consistently as policy, the socialist everyman on the third level would have followed and supported such a policy of change not only without reservations but indeed joyfully and enthusiastically.

It follows that the present impasse in post-communist transition is not at all a natural, let alone inevitable, phenomenon. The potential for making a decisive breakthrough to a radical policy of changing socialism into capitalism, and quite a strong one, is there and begs for its realization. Indeed, except for the seasoned and by now largely obsolete *nomenklatura apparatchiks,* no one in the entire post-communist world wishes to go back to the old days of "mature socialism." In Russia alone, the combined data of the opinion polls, elections, and referenda shows that no more than 12-14 percent of the adult population are nostalgic about the communist past and that another 8-10 percent are bemoaning the loss of the empire (*derzhava*) and the U.S.S.R.'s superpower status (*sverkhderzhava*) without sympathizing with communism and the old regime at all. The rest, that is about 76-80 percent, are ready to embrace western style capitalism in one form or another. And, of course, even a greater percentage of people value their newly acquired freedom very highly and are determined not to give it up, whatever it takes.[2] If they still continue, though to an ever decreasing degree, to stick to the remnants of the total state, it is because they see as yet no better alternative—the government has so far failed to provide such an alternative, and they are wise enough to ignore the calls of the political charlatans preaching restorationist ideas of the communist-fascist variety.

As a result, people in their daily lives start ignoring the government and lose interest in its ever vacillating policies. On an ever increasing scale, they use their newly born freedom for taking their fate into their own hands and do not mind pursuing their specific interests and goals by defying official policies, regulations, and even the law. What we are witnessing today all over Russia is massive unauthorized privatization of industrial, financial, and trade enterprises, together with land which by law still remains the exclusive property of the state. This is often called "*nomenklatura* privatization," but it involves not only the *nomenklatura* but many more ordinary people, without whose cooperation and participation the *nomenklaturists* in present circumstances could hardly be as successful as they are in this quite massive drive for illicit privatization.

Parallel with such privatization, new, mainly unlicensed (or only partly licensed) business enterprises and initiatives of different kinds are proliferating in every Russian city, town, and even village. And, around these enterprises and initiatives, racketeering and similar private protection and extortion groups are building themselves up. Smuggling and money laundering activities are growing in scope as are the numbers of people involved and the corruption of public officials. A new socioeconomic system based on people's freewheeling venturing for personal gain is thus being spontaneously formed, and although this process is taking place mainly outside the framework of law, very soon the thus newly created social structures will start craving legal and political recognition. At this point the government will start experiencing true public pressure for proceeding with changes in a swift manner and then will have no choice but, at least in a "tailing" manner, to start institutionalizing the spontaneous public initiatives "from bellow," independently of whether it had any consistent ideas on how to go about this business or not.

Meanwhile, the processes described above are being naturally accompanied by the country's ever progressing political fragmentation. Local authorities, directly facing and being the first to deal with all these spontaneous social developments, act with regard to them as they find fit, not as the central government wants them to, and, when finding it necessary or merely opportune, publicly dissociate themselves from the central government by unilaterally declaring their particular region or territory a sovereign republic, a free city or whatever is in their view best for accomplishing such a dissociation. In Russia life is taking its natural course, but without the government's cooperation in legitimizing that course, it acquires a dangerously destructive and to a large measure a criminal character, plunging the country into an ever greater social and economic chaos within which the government becomes increasingly irrelevant. The transition to capitalism may be, of course, accomplished in this spontaneous, destructively chaotic way, too, but the amount of time such a transition will take and the price it is going to exact from more than one generation of Russians will be enormous. If only Yeltsin and his team had the correct ideas on how to start organizing the transition to capitalism from above, and also the guts for resolutely going ahead with the business of translating these ideas into real life, they could spare their people a lot of suffering and misery, and also relieve the rest of the world from the necessity of dealing with the globally destabilizing consequences which that protracted suffering and misery in Russia will inevitably cause.

The real crisis in post-communist lands is thus not political and even not economic; it is, in my view, first and foremost, a *crisis of ideas*—ideas on how to ensure the transition from monolithic socialism to pluralistic capitalism without inflicting excessive social damage. The economic and political crises in the post-communist lands which we are witnessing today with such consternation are, in fact, mainly the direct result of that crisis of ideas. And these external crises will most likely continue unabated until either a set of consistent and sufficiently radical ideas on how resolutely to break with the socialist past is elaborated and then succinctly, with full conviction and commitment, translated into the respective governments' implementable strategies or until political fragmentation and complete breakdown of law and order spontaneously starts generating a new social and political system from below, with this process inevitably engendering the right ideas on the transition process for a successful government of the day to catch up with and follow as policy.

One should not, however, blame too strongly the post-communist governments for not having found and formulated the right ideas for the transition. Such a transition is unprecedented in history and there is neither experience to base such ideas upon nor any preceding ideas to adapt to the new circumstances and then to follow. As the popular Russian humorist Mikhail Zhvanetsky once said, "It is easy to make fish soup out of an aquarium, but no one has yet found a way to make an aquarium out of fish soup."[3] Indeed, not only the post-communist governments but no one in the entire world—East or West, North or South—could claim that he/she knows the right strategy for insuring the transition from socialism to capitalism. This does not mean, however, that one should not try to think about such a strategy or refuse to come forward with new ideas on how best this unprecedented transition could be accomplished. After all, any human society, however perverse, is not exactly fish soup. It is still more of an aquarium where, by a due effort, living conditions could be significantly improved and even brought to normal standards. And if the main problem of such a "fish-soup like aquarium" is a crisis of ideas, there is probably no other way of solving this crisis but by constantly putting forward new ideas critical of and distinct from the previous ones.

III. The Hillsdale Plan: Origins

One among the many ideas on how to secure the transition to free market capitalism in post-communist societies is the so-called Hillsdale Plan. As one of the participants in the elaboration of this plan, I would not dare to claim that it is superior to other such plans or that it is substantially better than what the respective governments are trying to do in implementing their plans of privatization and marketization. What I would, however, venture to say is that our plan is markedly different from the other plans, either the ones discussed in academic literature or the ones put forward by political parties, their activists and writers, as well as by the governments themselves, and as such it stands unique. I believe that by virtue of that uniqueness the Hillsdale plan deserves due attention and consideration. I also believe that since the ideas of our plan have never been tried and the results of trying to implement other ideas were so far pretty meager, the original Hillsdale Plan with some amendments necessitated by the passage of time could still be used as a viable foundation for elaborating a practical strategy for the transition to capitalism in the former republics of the U.S.S.R., e.g., in Russia, and, perhaps, in some other post-communist lands.

In its initial rough shape the Hillsdale plan evolved spontaneously three years ago, during the 1990 Ludwig von Mises Lecture Series. A delegation of prominent economists from Lithuania, a country which only a month before the event proclaimed its independence from the U.S.S.R., was invited to share with us their plans for economic reforms. The discussion of these plans continued in many informal sessions. They lasted late into the night every day for about a week and were very active, some times even heated. Among the most active participants projecting original ideas on how best to privatize the Lithuanian economy, on how to reform its finances and banking, on how to proceed with the land reform, and on other similar topics, were Hillsdale professors Charles Van Eaton, Gary Wolfram and Richard Ebeling, as well as University of Georgia economist George Selgin and a number of other scholars participating in a special symposium of the Ludwig von Mises Lecture Series.

It was during these discussions that the Hillsdale Plan was born. Suddenly, close to the end of the proceedings, it became clear to all participants that a quite consistent and interesting concept on how to make the transition to capitalism in Lithuania possible had evolved as result of all these animated debates.

Our Lithuanian guests were also strongly impressed with these informal discussions. They invited George Roche, president of Hillsdale College, to visit Lithuania and inaugurate the newly founded Free Market Institute there. George Roche made two important speeches in Lithuania in which he encouraged his listeners to use the opportunity of a new beginning to boldly and unhesitantly establish an economic system truly free of government interference and encroachment, a system which would be able to demonstrate to the entire world the enormous advantages of a genuinely free market and the perniciousness of socialist planning and governmental regulation of the economy which increasingly permeate the economic systems of the Western world. George Roche's speeches were translated into Lithuanian and published by a leading Lithuanian cultural periodical.[4]

They received wide attention in the country and also served as the theoretical foundation for further developing the Hillsdale Plan.

Later, in summer of 1990, at the invitation of one of the country's leading commercial banks, I visited Lithuania in order to present the Hillsdale Plan to various academic, business, and political audiences, via radio, television, and lectures, as well as interviews and articles published in Lithuania's mass media. At the time of my visit to Lithuania, I had at my disposal, in addition to George Roche's Lithuanian speeches, a fundamental academic article on the problems of privatization of Lithuania's economy produced by Professor Gary Wolfram[5] and also the rich and novel ideas on the subject by another Hillsdale professor, Richard Ebeling, who was generous enough to share and discuss them with me on a regular, almost daily basis throughout 1990 and beyond. Roche's speeches, Wolfram's article and Ebeling's creative ideas have formed the foundations of the Hillsdale Plan for which I considered myself a mere consenting spokesman.

In January, 1991 Professor Ebeling and I traveled to Lithuania and Moscow, where we together continued to do what I was less ably doing alone when visiting Lithuania (and also Moscow and St. Petersburg) in the summer of 1990. On this occasion, we were able to address the parliaments of Lithuania and Russia and their various commissions and groups of deputies trying to persuade them to adopt the Hillsdale Plan as a guide for the privatization schemes they were discussing at the time. At the request of a group of members of the economic reform commission of the Russian parliament, I prepared a draft for Russia's privatization law; at the request of one of Russia's industrial giants, the chemical factory *Azot,* professors Ebeling and Van Eaton prepared a plan for that factory's privatization.

In the summer of 1991 Professor Ebeling and I went back to Lithuania and Moscow to participate in a number of important conferences and congresses. We also continued lecturing, publishing, and appearing on radio and television. I went on to continue that mission in Poland, Hungary, and in what was then still Czechoslovakia.

One article which we produced together was published in the Lithuanian magazine *Politika*.[6] Others we published separately. I was writing and publishing mainly in Russian and Lithuanian (but many of my writings were translated and quite widely published in Poland, Hungary, and Bulgaria, too),[7] that is for local consumption, while Professor Ebeling published his in English both in Lithuania and in this country for the attention of the professional economists and other interested academics here and there.[8]

Unfortunately, the practical results of our propaganda efforts were rather meager. Perhaps the ideas were too radical for most state officials or Soviet-educated academics to espouse and follow. But, I think, this obstacle could have been overcome if we had enough time and resources to do the job properly. I think, our campaign advocating the Hillsdale Plan was too episodic and too weak to stand a chance of becoming a real success. We were only two people spending no more than a matter of days in countries where hundreds of other Western economists, academics, and officials from all kinds of influential institutions were preaching full-time in a massive and ubiquitous endeavor a message distinctly at odds with ours. It is no surprise that our voices were drowned out by that powerful and constant choir of Keynesian and Samuelsonian economic manipulators, especially because behind the voices of that choir the listeners were able to perceive lurking not only ideas but also big money. With our duo this was clearly not the case, and thus there was no big incentive to follow the message of our song.

IV. The Hillsdale Plan: Substance

Let me now, briefly sum up the main ideas of the Hillsdale Plan.

I think it would be fair to say that our concern with the privatization program was subordinated to what we regarded as the main task of the reform—the minimization of the state, the outright liquidation of all of its uniquely Soviet-type gigantic institutions dealing with planning, supplying, and managing the economy. Privatization was for us not so much an end in itself as a means to the main end—the end of dismantling the Soviet totalitarian state, of evacuating political power from the realm of the thus recreated civil society, of the institution, as a result, of an authentic *Rechtsstaat*. This is what attracted me, a lawyer and a political scientist who does not know much about economics at all, to participate in the Hillsdale Plan in the first place. And this is also, I think, why the Hillsdale Plan was not very popular with the Lithuanian, Russian, and other countries' planners of economic reforms, all of whom, even those with scholarly identities, were inevitably state officials.

Our privatization plan was divided into two parts, the way privatization was later conducted in former Czechoslovakia. The smaller enterprises—such as small to medium retail stores, restaurants, launderettes, repair shops, handicrafts, other similar small to medium manufacturing outlets, etc.—had to be sold directly in auctions which would accept preliminary bids in sealed envelopes equal to or exceeding the state accorded value (in Russian called *balansovaya stoimost'*, the balance value) of the particular enterprise. The medium and large enterprises would have to be first converted into stockholding companies and then the ownership of the stock issued for each separate enterprise in the sum of that enterprise's state accorded (balance) value transferred from the state to the enterprise itself. The enterprise would thus receive the rights of "self-ownership" as a legal person and, after the transfer of these rights to it, would be reconstituted as an independent corporate entity led by a board of directors and supervised by a newly formed board of trustees.

In contrast to all other plans, the Hillsdale Plan was one of instantaneous and truly total privatization. According to it, no industrial, agrarian, financial, or any other service enterprise remained in the state's hands. We only allowed, though quite grudgingly, for the Central Bank to be a part of the state's system, as well as the railways, electric energy supply networks, some other communal and public services which could temporarily continue under the state's management.

It was also of crucial importance for the Hillsdale Plan to make sure that the stock was transferred to the single enterprise and not to any concerns, trusts, productive unions (*ob'edinenie*) and other intermediary (between the enterprise and the state) bodies to which more than one single enterprise was subordinated. In our plan, such intermediary economic organizations were to be dissolved by the sheer process of share transfer to the single enterprise, and to no one above or outside of it. Later, when on the market, the enterprises could, for economic reasons, start forming trusts, concerns, and other similar unions again. But, it seemed to us, that in the beginning the method of according property rights exclusively to single enterprises was the only reliable way for breaking up monopolies, encouraging competition, and promoting self-sufficiency of smaller economic units.

According to our plan, the single enterprise, when accepting the stock into its ownership, had to sign to that effect a debtor's contract with the state in which the time for the enterprise's full repayment to the state of the nominal value of the stock received (usually, about three to five years) had to be stipulated. The enterprise's failure to repay this "foundation" debt to the state in the agreed time would make it insolvent with bankruptcy proceedings to follow. This is to say that in our plan the enterprise's survival depended on its ability to sell its stock on the stock exchange. The organization of stock exchanges and other institutions (such as investment companies) serving the capital market would be left to the enterprises and other private participants of transactions taking place in this market to deal with. The state had to be excluded from this process altogether.

This way of proceeding with the privatization of medium and large state enterprises, in our view, would have accomplished immediately, virtually in one single go and in its entirety, what one could call the "primary stage" of privatization—the stage at which all enterprises would be transformed into independent corporate entities, fully divorced from the state. In their new corporate capacity, the enterprises would enter (furthermore, form) the free market where, in order to survive and succeed, they would have to sell with profit their products and also—dependent of course on the success of these sales—to find for themselves their true owners, i.e., persons willing to buy their shares. It is in the thus established free market that what one could call "secondary privatization" starts taking place. In this secondary stage, the enterprises would either find for themselves real private owners, the stockholders, or, if they failed in that endeavor, go into liquidation. This process could take up to five or even more years and, in fact, it would never stop, as stock constantly changes hands and no enterprise operating on the free market could ever be entirely immune to bankruptcy.

Before the enterprise's stock was to be put on sale through stock exchanges and other public channels, the employees of that enterprise had to be given the right of buying its stock at the nominal price (that is without paying commission or other overheads, but not at artificial discount prices) directly from the enterprise. During the first six months of free sales of the enterprise's shares at the stock exchange and through other public channels, the right of buying them was to be accorded only to the respective country's nationals and enterprises. After this period of privileged buying, the stock had to be made available for purchasing to everyone equally, e.g. to foreign nationals and firms, too.

It follows from the above that the Hillsdale Plan does not foresee either voucher privatization or any privileged distribution of stock among the enterprise's employees and managers. In the latter case, as was pointed out above, the enterprise's employees and managers are given the possibility of priority buying at the nominal price of as much stock as they like, directly from the enterprise. As for the vouchers, our proposal was quite different from the standard concepts of "voucher-privatization."

To be sure, we foresaw the issue of vouchers, too, but only for the limited sum of 40 percent of the difference between the state accorded summary value of all enterprises assigned for privatization and the total sum of savings held by the country's nationals in their bank accounts. We thought that on the whole people would be willing to invest into the successful enterprises' stocks more money than they had saved in their bank accounts. We also wanted to leave enough stock for firms and enterprises as well as for foreign investors to buy on the stock exchanges. The 60 percent difference between the summary value of all stock and the overall sum of peoples' savings catered in our calculations for all these purposes quite adequately. Vouchers issued for the remaining 40 percent of that sum had to go to the private individuals in order to enable and encourage them to buy more stock, but not in the way of their equal distribution among all citizens, as it is now done in Russia, the Czech Republic, most recently in Bulgaria and elsewhere, where every citizen, even a new-born child, is accorded one voucher with equal nominal value, which, for example, in the Russian case is determined as ten thousand rubles in 1991 prices. (The Russians calculated this amount as constituting in the overall sum of the vouchers issued percent of the total value of enterprises releasable for privatization).

What we wanted to do was to combine the distribution of vouchers with the provision of social assistance to the most needy members of society, the ones, for example, whose income is below of, or equal to, the officially established minimal standard of living. The overall sum attributed to issuing in vouchers would be thus divided by the number of people "in need of welfare" with each such individual receiving one voucher bearing the equal nominal value determined by the above calculations. In our plan, these vouchers had to be issued together with the transfer of stock to the enterprises, but they could be realized, that is exchanged for real stock, only in stock exchanges and through other public channels selling stock. This is to say that, being issued in the "primary stage" of privatization, vouchers could be used for acquiring stock only in its "secondary stage." (That would give enough time for establishing a market for vouchers which later would be able naturally to expand to shares and other capital goods.)

What I would like to stress here is the fact that by proceeding with privatization in this way not only is the market economy being created practically overnight, but also the state's economic apparatus is simultaneously rendered obsolete, with the economically relevant functions it used to perform (and still is performing) being without transfers or delays also privatized by the way of creating in the private sector stock and commodity exchanges, marketing and wholesale agencies, sales mediation bureaus and other similar service institutions.

The state's participation in the initial process of "primary privatization"—the transfer of stock to, conclusion of contracts with, and supervision of timely payments for the transferred stock, by the enterprises—is to be handled in Hillsdale Plan's provisions exclusively by the Ministry of Finance and its local divisions, that is the state's fiscal authority and the only state institution which in the conditions of free market is, anyway, bound to grow and become more complex in its functions.

Simultaneously with such a total and instantaneous privatization—privatization accomplished in one go and throughout the whole economy—all prices and wages have had to be freed, too. Price controls, this last vestige of the state's direct management of the economy, must be rescinded once and for all, so that no loophole, allowing for even a partial or conditional restoration of economic management by the state, is left . And, of course, the state has to be also deprived of any authority to interfere into the process of free wages' settlements by the employers and employees.

Along and simultaneously with "primary" privatization and freeing of prices and wages, the local currency has to be made fully (not only internally) convertible, too, without any "justifiable" delays allowed to stand in the way of this financial reform. As long as the local currency is not fully convertible, the economy will refuse properly to serve the legal domestic markets, choosing instead the ones in which real, not phoney, money could be made and thus causing profound economic disruption. To insure the stabilization of the local currency after it was made convertible, the Hillsdale Plan proposed to attach it to a stable foreign currency, for example, to the U.S. dollar or the German mark (or to both simultaneously), according to that chosen foreign currency(ies) the status of legal tender, alongside with the local currency.

The money the state is to receive from enterprises for the stock that it transferred into their ownership, has to be allocated, according to the Hillsdale Plan, partly for social security compensations to those whose income falls below the established minimal standard of living, and partly for the personnel retraining needs. In the Hillsdale Plan Milton Friedman's idea of negative taxation,[9] when slightly adjusted to the specific circumstances of the post-communist situation, is considered to provide the best method for organizing social security payments to the needy.

Friedman links negative taxation—"a single comprehensive program of income supplements in cash"—to the positive income tax and specifically to the regulations providing for "personal allowances" establishing the amounts of nontaxable income. The peculiarities of the tax regulations in post-communist lands, which would hardly change in substance before other, more profound economic changes took place, would make such a linkage absolutely impractical. Therefore, instead of linking negative taxation to positive income tax, we proposed to link it to the minimal standard of living. The latter, according to our Plan, has to be calculated for every single day, very much like currency exchange rates which are calculated daily, too. With such data at hand, there would be not much difficulty to determine whether a person's weekly or monthly income matched the minimal standard of living for exactly the same period of time for which it has been received. If it did not, the person in question would be entitled to receive from the state the difference in cash. This way of according negative tax is deemed by the plan temporary, lasting only until the transition had been settled and privatized enterprises had paid off their 'foundation debt' to the state. But the negative tax itself is recommended as permanent. In time, with the taxation system brought into correspondence with the new economic conditions, it is to be separated from the minimal standard of living, linked, as the original proposal suggests, with the positive income tax, and used as the sole means of welfare provision by the state. The post-communist states have a unique chance to escape the trap of the welfare state into which most of the Western states have already fallen, and this chance lies in their consistent and permanent usage of negative taxation.

For the transition period, negative taxation provides, in our view, the best remedy for making the so-called "shock therapy" associated with it optimally therapeutic and minimally shocking. It also most effectively dispels the paralyzing horror stories about the unbearable price one has to pay for the radical transition from socialism to capitalism. The price, though not negligible, is, as we tried to demonstrate, quite a bearable one; it is, in any case, much less of a price than the really unbearable one of procrastination and indecision about radically dismantling the socialist system once and for all, which the post-communist nations are currently so dearly paying.

One of the most numerous categories of the likely users of negative taxation will certainly be the trainees for new professions. There will be quite a lot of them, as in post-communist countries a great many of the professions necessary for a modern society normally to function simply do not exist or are in extremely short supply. In post-communist societies, to name but a few of such "missing professions," there are, for example, no real estate or travel agents, no probation officers or financial advisers, no credit providers or investment specialists, no salesmen or insurance brokers; the absence of capital markets and wholesale trade-marks more fields of potential ample employment into by now non-existent and special training requiring professions. In ridiculously short supply are bankers, lawyers, all kinds of contractors, even shop assistants; and those who perform these functions now, in order to be able to continue their professional activities in the emerging new, Western-type social and economic order are in great need of a very thorough retraining, too.

The original Hillsdale Plan sketched out above could thus be briefly summarized in the following four points:

1) An instantaneous transfer on credit of the state's property rights over every single medium and large enterprise to that enterprise itself as to an independent corporate entity; direct and prompt sale by the state of its small to medium size enterprises to the highest bidder in auctions;

2) Simultaneous freeing of all prices and wages;

3) Simultaneous transformation of the local currency into a fully convertible currency;

4) Introduction of negative taxation.

The Hillsdale Plan did not, however, end with this proposal which basically concentrated on state property in industry, trade, finance, and other services but did not encompass the formally non-state 'socialist cooperative' property, e.g., the property of the collective farms. We have outlined some basic proposals on these issues, too. Among the issues dealt with in other parts of the Hillsdale Plan were: 1) the agrarian (land) and collective farms' reform; 2) the ways of attracting foreign capital investment; 3) the bank reform and monetary emission rights; 4) the incentives for formation of new private businesses; 5) the provision of legal foundations for regulating the functioning of a free market and private ownership based economy; and 6) the basic principles of taxation.

I am mentioning these six points only to give the reader a better idea of the scope of the Hillsdale Plan. I am not going to deal with these points at any length or depth because of the considerations of time and space, but also because of their derivative nature. The six points mentioned above follow from the basic idea on how the main breakthrough to a market based civil society in post-communist lands should be accomplished. The chief purpose of this paper was to explain this basic idea first, and, on that basis, to initiate a further, and, perhaps, a more detailed discussion of the issues involved. The practical ways of dealing with privatization in post-communist lands will be presenting the scholarly community with a lot of different debatable issues for yet some time to come, and I would like to see the ideas of the Hillsdale Plan figuring in such debates prominently and developing further through exposure to continuous discussion, critical comments, and challenging counter-proposals.

To be entirely frank, I still believe that the Hillsdale Plan offers the best solution for the problems of transition from socialism to private property and market based civil society; and, moreover, that all the other plans tried for accomplishing that transition in various post-communist lands have not as yet made our Plan obsolete. When the attempts at applying all the other plans are exhausted and new alternative plans are being sought by the local protagonists of the transition again, the Hillsdale Plan will, I hope, stand ready for all those seriously considering a resolute rejection of the remnants of socialism and a committed, unhesitant pursuit of "capitalist construction" to use and make a reality.

Notes

[1]On the "other plans," see: Janos Kornai, *The Road to a Free Economy: Shifting From a Socialist System* (New York: W.W. Norton, 1990); id., *The Socialist System: The Political Economy of Communism* (Princeton, N.J.: Princeton University Press, 1992); Kazimierz Z. Poznanski ed., *Constructing Capitalism: The Reemergence of Civil Society and Liberal Economy in the Post-Communist World* (Boulder: Westview Press, 1992); Michael Keren and Gur Offer eds., *Trials of Transition: Reform in the Former Communist Bloc* (Boulder: Westview Press, 1992); Bruno Delago, et al., *Privatization and Entrepreneurship in Post-Socialist Countries* (New York: St. Martin's Press, 1992); Shafiqul Islam & Michael Mandelbaum, *Making Markets: Economic Transformation in Eastern Europe and the Post-Soviet States* (New York: Council on Foreign Relations Press, 1993), and a few more similar collections.

[2]This data on public opinion in Russia is based on my continuous comparative analysis of monthly opinion polls conducted by two authoritative poll-taking Russian institutions, The Russian Academy of Sciences' Institute of Public Opinion (CIOM, headed by the prominent Russian sociologist Yuriy Levada) and the Institute of the Sociology of Parliamentarism (headed by Nuzgar Betaneli) since the spring of 1991. I supplemented these with data provided by the results of the June 12, 1991 presidential election and the April 25, 1993 referendum, as well as with data of some relevant results of opinion polls conducted not on a regular basis but by special commission. One of them, jointly conducted by the Russian Academy of Sciences' Institute of Sociology and

Virginia University in September 1992, deserves special attention. According to its results, only 12.6 percent declared their opposition to privatization, while 83 percent were not simply in favor of it but declared their firm support for the country's transition to full-blown capitalism. Among the latter group, interestingly, a substantial proportion were people bitterly critical of the Yeltsin regime. They apparently were the same people who in other sections of the poll accused Yeltsin of mismanaging the reforms and of thus permanently relegating Russia to backwardness and dependency on the developed Western world. (For a summary of that poll's results, see: Vladimir Loyevetsky, "Obshchestvennoe mnenie—o delakh privatnykh" [Public Opinion—on Things Private], in *Moskovskie novosti* [Moscow News], No. 40, October 4, 1992).

[3] I am indebted to Professor Martin Malia for drawing my attention to the Zhvanetsky story containing this expression.

[4] See: *Svyturys,* No. 4, February 1991, 21ff.

[5] At the time, Wolfram's article was available in the form of a conference paper. It was published as G. Wolfram, "Lithuania and Its Transition to a Market Economy: How To Begin," in Robert W. McGee (ed.), *The Market Solution to Economic Development in Eastern Europe* (Lewiston, N.Y.: The Edwin Mellen Press, 1992). Wolfram developed his Hillsdale Plan related ideas in later writings, too; see, for example, his "A Note on Converting the Ruble," in *The Freeman,* Vol. 41, No. 1, January, 1991, and "Real Transition to a Market Economy," in *The Economist of Lithuania,* No. 2, 1992.

[6] No. 22, 1991.

[7] The most fundamental and comprehensive presentation of my ideas on the Hillsdale Plan was published in Russian by the "thick" magazine *Grani* (Facets), in Vol. XLVI, No. 161, 1991, as "Privatizatsiya" (Privatization); appended to the text of the article was also my draft of the Law on Privatization, written at the request of, and submitted to, the Russian Parliament. All my other quite numerous publications on the subject were either derivatives or various versions of the text published in *Grani.*

[8] Among Ebeling's numerous publications on the subject, I would single out his *Privatizing the Lithuanian Economy: Proposals and Possibilities* (a separate pamphlet, published by The Future of Freedom Foundation in Denver, CO, 1991) and "Economic Reform in Russia. The First Year" (in *News and Views,* Vol.1, No.2, Spring, 1993). See also his "A Program for Privatization and Market Reform in Lithuania," in *The Economist of Lithuania,* Fall, 1991.

[9]For a popular but pretty adequate explanation of the concept, see, Milton Friedman and Rose Friedman, *Free to Choose* (London: Secker and Warburg, 1980), especially 120–126.

Elena Bonner

The Rebirth of Democracy in the Former Soviet Empire

The April 1993 Referendum

Russia has been going through one more critical stage of development in the difficult transition to democracy, a stage that is at once cause for optimism and pessimism. In April of 1993, key members of the Congress of People's Deputies did their utmost to ruin the national referendum that was in essence meant to determine the fate of the policies and presidency of Boris Yeltsin. Specifically, they attempted to rig the questions on the referendum ballot so as to ensure a vote of no confidence. But their efforts failed spectacularly, and once again the Russian people unequivocally demonstrated their loyalty to President Yeltsin and to the cause of democracy.

So much for the good news. The serious problem of deteriorating relations between the Congress of People's Deputies and the president remained. The current deputies were elected in March 1990, when the Communist Party was still in power. Some "experts" have claimed that they were elected by fair and democratic means, but this is not true. As a result, the overwhelming majority were old Party functionaries and members of the *nomenklatura*. Sixty-two percent—i.e., 639 out of a total of 1,033 deputies—consistently opposed democratic reforms. Just before the referendum, 618 actually voted to impeach Yeltsin. Only 38 percent—394 deputies—consistently supported the president and the policies of reform. Each group spent most of its time battling to win over wavering deputies. In this environment, it was highly unlikely that the Congress of People's Deputies could achieve any substantive reform.

An Anticonstitutional Crisis

Russia desperately needed—and needed soon if more violence was to be averted—a new written constitution. Without one, it would see more of what happened in the streets of Moscow on May 1, when deputies upset by the outcome of the referendum incited massive street violence in Moscow—the likes of which hadn't been seen since 1917 when the Bolsheviks used the same tactics in trying to come to power. In this case, tragically, over 500 hundred people were injured and one person was killed.

Democratic, pro-constitutional forces squandered their last political victory in August, 1991 after the failed coup attempt when it would have been feasible to painlessly adopt a new constitution and to change the membership of the Congress. They must not squander future victories. In early 1993, you could not have drummed up much interest in a new constitution, but after the successful referendum, it was on everyone's mind. On April 29, the Yeltsin government unveiled its proposed version of a new constitution. It seemed to be the most democratic and the most adequate response yet to the needs of the nation. (In my opinion, it still gives too much power to the president.)

The first and primary chapter in the Yeltsin constitution guaranteed the civil rights of all citizens. The second chapter outlined a federalist system in which autonomous republics, regions, provinces, and local governments retained a large degree of independence. (Anti-reform elements in Congress strongly opposed this provision. They would have rather followed the old Soviet model of centralized power. But Yeltsin was adamant that the only way to save Russia was to allow decentralization.) In addition, the Yeltsin constitution called for a whole new structure for the national government, featuring a two-chamber parliament with wide representation and four-year term limits. It also guaranteed the inviolability of private property rights, including land ownership.

The constitution Russians had been forced to live under was a relic of communism. It was written in 1936, and for decades it was known simply as the "Stalin Constitution." Then in 1978, when it was revised to further tighten the grip of the Communist Party, it was dubbed the "Brezhnev Constitution." During 1992 and the first half of 1993, 342 amendments to the "Brezhnev Constitution" were passed by the Congress of People's Deputies, but this only succeeded in making matters more confusing and contradictory and forestalled any genuine improvement. Instead of serving as the supreme law of the land, the constitution was still the instrument of self-serving politicians. Some observers, therefore, characterized this stage of Russia's development as a constitutional crisis, but in reality it was an anti-constitutional crisis.

The Nuclear Arms Issue

There was another crisis looming on the horizon for Russia in 1993. In an interview a few days before the April 25 referendum, Ruslan Khasbulatov, the chairman of the Supreme Soviet of the Congress of People's Deputies, was asked by the Western press about the ratification of the START agreements. He replied categorically that the Congress would not ratify any arms treaty until Andrei Kozyrev, minister of foreign affairs and one of Yeltsin's staunchest supporters, was fired or forced to resign. In other words, arms reduction became a hostage that could be ransomed only for a certain political price. The Congress was filled with deputies like Khasbulatov who think and behave this way. They displayed a deadly combination of infantilism, belligerence, and irresponsibility that Western leaders should continue to heed, especially when they call for all Soviet nuclear weapons to be transferred to Russia. Until Russia becomes a stable democratic state with leaders who pledge to abide by the law rather than their own whims, no weapons should be transferred. Just imagine for a moment that the people who were behind the May 1 violence in Moscow suddenly had total political power backed up by total control of the only nuclear arsenal in the Commonwealth of Independent States (CIS).

Russia and the CIS

Some say that the real hope for peace and progress lies in once again uniting all the former Soviet republics under the banner of one government. But their ethnic roots, histories and cultures are far too different. Nothing short of World War III would ever unite them again. But the new Russian constitution could be an enormous benefit for all CIS countries. Leonid Kravchuk, president of the Ukraine, acknowledged as much when he endorsed Yeltsin just before the April 1993 referendum. The fact that he chose to make his support public marked a watershed in the post-communist era, for up until then CIS solidarity had been a sham. This unprecedented overture signaled that a new era of cooperation between CIS countries had begun.

Western Aid

There is one more issue that I want to mention, the issue of Western aid. First, it is vital that this aid be distributed equitably to all CIS countries. Russia should not receive a disproportionate share; she is not, contrary to what you may see in the news, on the verge of starvation. But there are regions in the former U.S.S.R. that are hunger-stricken. These are the ones that are caught up in armed conflict such as Tadgikistan; or the ones that have been devastated by natural disaster like Kyrgyzstan, which suffered an earthquake that destroyed the harvest. There is also Armenia, which has been subjected to blockade since 1989; Ingushetia with thousands of homeless as a result of conflict with Osseria; and Abkhasia, which is in need of aid because of its on going war with Georgia.

Second, the Jackson Amendment of the 1970s should be revived. No U.S. aid should be given to countries where human rights are routinely violated. Other nations should follow this example when formulating their own aid policies. Unless aid is linked directly to human rights, the West has no leverage to effect change—it is only subsidizing injustice and tyranny.

Third, Western aid should not be the most important or the only method of helping. Money, even when it amounts to billions of dollars, cannot overcome every problem. Sometimes it can even make problems worse. If the West really wishes to help, it should support efforts in CIS countries to establish democratic constitutions that will guarantee human rights, a stable currency, private property, foreign investments, free trade, and the rule of law. Western creditors should also consider postponing debt payments, especially since the debts in question were incurred by Yeltsin's communist predecessors.

The Generation That Is the Future

I said at the outset that this stage in Russia's transition to democracy is cause for optimism and pessimism. Ultimately, I think optimism will triumph. Why am I so sure? It is not just because of the huge turnout for the April 1993 referendum, even though that turnout was phenomenal by any standards. It is mainly because I have seen who turned out. The biggest pro-Yeltsin, pro-reform group was comprised of Russian men and women between 20 and 35 years old. These young people are better educated and better trained than ever before and they have something that is totally new in Russian society: a global mentality. Moreover, they outnumber those who oppose reform—the retired, the veterans of war, of labor and of the Communist Party. These young people are Russia's future. They will not give up on freedom, and we should not give up on them.

George Roche

The Road to Freedom

Morality According to Karl Marx

The biggest story of our times is this: Communism is dying. But perhaps the most striking feature of its demise is that it is not accompanied by much of a celebration of the triumph of capitalism in the West. You would expect countless books, articles and spokesmen proclaiming victory for the free market. You would expect a massive intellectual defense and explanation of capitalist ideas—and perhaps some crowing about how much better they are. You also would expect political leaders in the West to redouble their efforts to expand liberty. True, there has been some of each of these, but there has been no concerted effort to claim victory.

The near-silence is ominous. It is as if we had achieved great ends with evil means and ought to be ashamed rather than exultant at our success. This guilty feeling is itself a communist hangover. We should be rid of it once and for all, or Marx will have the last laugh. Moreover, we must seek to understand the cause of the communist demise. Until we understand the cause, we will not be able to heal the frightful wounds communism leaves behind, and we will ourselves remain in peril of repeating the same mistakes.

We do know that without a doubt the economic performance of communism has been dismal everywhere it has been tried. Communism simply cannot compete with free markets. But it was not economic failure that really killed communism in Eastern Europe or the former Soviet Union or that is in the process of finishing it off in Latin America and Asia. We would be greatly mistaken if we assumed that people in closed societies only want more consumer goods. Certainly they would like more and better food, housing, clothes and appliances—wouldn't we all? But it is not a yearning for mere possessions that moves them. After all, they have from the beginning endured economic disaster and terrible privation.

Ultimately, the death of communism has been brought about by its own spiritual failure. The triumph of "capitalism" is equally a spiritual victory, but we in the West have been slow to recognize it as such. I put "capitalism" in quotation marks because it is a Marxist coinage and a hate word. It is also bad coinage—all systems are necessarily capitalist, because they all have to allocate capital. But everyone is pretty much agreed about its Marxist and principal meaning: a free market system based on the ownership of private property and the free exchange of goods. I am happy to accept this meaning and insofar as I use the term, that is what I mean by it.

When I say capitalist ideas are better, I mean precisely in their spiritual dimension. Of course they are more efficient; everybody knows that. It is hardly worth saying. What few see, however, is their moral goodness. We are still blinded by that awful bit of Marxian theory called "the theory of surplus value" that has for more than a century stood moral law on its head. The theory long ago disappeared from formal economics (even the communists found it an embarrassment), but its false conclusion is still with us. It is summarized by an economic encyclopedia (which mentioned the "notoriety" Marx gave it) as follows: "Profit is unpaid labor appropriated by capitalists as a consequence of the institution of private property."

In other words, according to Marx, the capitalist system alone causes poverty (by paying low wages), unemployment and periodic depressions. Private property is bad. Rent and interest are stolen from workers. Capitalists are all greedy, grasping, mean, and exploitative. By extension, wealth is considered ill-gotten and tainted (this has led many a rich person to finance revolutionary causes out of guilt for earning or inheriting wealth). We need only document real cases of nasty capitalists and exploited workers (of which there are, of course, many), ignoring everything else, to make the case seem valid. But it is nonsense, and the evidence against it, in both theory and fact, is overwhelming.

Marx's theory is the perfect excuse for every personal failure in the market. With it, you can blame anything on the capitalist (your boss, your foreman, society, the system). You didn't succeed because you were being exploited and stolen from. It is human nature to want to excuse one's own mistakes, and here Marx offers absolution for any failing, free for the asking. You don't even have to repent. But there is a price: To believe it, you have to learn to hate. The "bourgeoisie" is to the communist dictators what the Jews were to Hitler: the hate object used to "unite the people." Totalitarianism always requires a permanent enemy, a group to hate. The hate object must be an abstract class (individuals are too concrete and too well known to each other), and it must be "evil." Once a would-be dictator persuades you to hate this class, you are his slave. He is in complete control. You even stop thinking for yourself. It is only a short step beyond this to justify or to take part in genocide—the gulag or the Holocaust.

It is little remembered now, but Marx first advertised his theories as more economically efficient. They got nowhere. In fact, they were drubbed by experience: Capitalism was booming and wages were rising rapidly when in the mid-19th century he published his predictions that workers would be reduced to poverty. Only when they lost the argument about efficiency did Marx and the communists turn to a moral argument, saying that capitalism was unjust. Only then did they prevail, for there was no rebuttal in moral terms. The claims of capitalist evils have been the whole strength of communism ever since and still pollute such intellectual swamps as Beijing, Ethiopia, and a number of American college campuses.

Morality in Econ 101

But capitalism is not unjust, nor it is unnatural or immoral; its structure and rules are as ethical as they are efficient. It is communism, on the other hand, that is unjust, unnatural, and immoral, as is finally becoming clear after the cruelest century in human memory—a century when nearly 170 million people sacrificed their lives, mainly on the altar of statism and socialist or communist ideology. Whereas socialism and communism appeal to hatred and envy, capitalism not only appeals to our moral instinct to help others, but harnesses our energies to that purpose and rewards most those who do the most for humanity.

All of us, you see, live in a whirl of activity that involves the transfer of goods and services. We sell our labor and produce, or rent and invest our capital, for money. With our money we buy food, clothing, shelter and the niceties of life. There are only two ways goods can be transferred: The first is one-sided and involuntary to one of the parties: One party takes what the other has, without giving anything of value for it. This is called stealing (or in some cases, taxes). Obviously, in such a one-sided transfer, the first party gains and the second party loses. It may look like a break-even transaction, but it is not; it reduces the value of the goods to both parties, and is a net loss to the nation. It also directs future behavior by both parties to less productive channels, adding to the net loss.

The second kind of transfer is two-sided: Both parties voluntarily agree to the exchange. Its key feature is that it is freely chosen. This, and this only, may be called an economic exchange; the word exchange even implies mutual consent. When we see why both parties agree, we have the key to the whole of modern economic science. It is simply human nature. Each of us is one of a kind, not only in mind and body, but in our talents, wants and goals. We each have a scale of values for what we want, how much we want it, and what we will do to get it. Moreover, our wants and goals change constantly: We want food when we are hungry, not right after a meal. We each know what is the best thing to do according to our particular needs at a given moment, and we act on our self-knowledge; nobody else knows, and nobody else can decide for us. No two of us ever have quite the same scale of values directing what we do.

You can easily see this theory in operation at a well-stocked cafeteria: Rarely will two people choose exactly the same meal. The differences between us are, as the saying goes, what make horse races—and the whole free market. We make different exchanges because we value things differently. You exchange your dollar for a loaf of bread because you value the bread more than the dollar. The baker agrees to the exchange because he values the bread less than the dollar. Such is the nature of all exchanges in the market, no matter how complicated they may seem in their details. It is invariably a matter of people trading something they value less for something they value more.

The principles we derive from this fact are so important that they figuratively make the world go round. First, both parties gain from the exchange. This refutes the notion that there is only so much wealth to go around, and, if somebody gets some of it, he has to take it away from somebody else. What hogwash! Wealth is constantly being produced and consumed. It is merely distributed through the marketplace. The more of it there is, the easier it gets for all of us to have some: This is simple supply and demand.

Second, the goods or services freely exchanged increase in value, because both parties value them more highly. Or, you can say that they move from less to more valuable usage through more efficient allocation. Free exchanges are a constant process of moving goods, capital, and labor to where they are most useful, making us all richer in the bargain.

The third principle is incentive. When we make a good exchange and are rewarded for it, we have a greater motive to do it again. Reward for our effort brings out our best in the marketplace. But when we are cheated out of what we earn or own by crime or confiscatory taxes, we lose interest in working so hard. Every dollar taken away is a disincentive to economic production.

But we don't necessarily abide by these principles here in the U.S., and that ought to serve as a warning to those in the postcommunist world who want to imitate us. By mid-1992, federal, state, and local governments were consuming 45 percent of the national income. That was before the election of President Clinton. Just imagine how that figure is bound to go up in the next few years. We are still a wealthy people, but no nation can survive forever so great and systematic an assault on its ability and incentive to produce. If our moral sense no longer tells us this, our gift for economics should. Every dollar we confiscate is devalued. The so-called transfer makes it worth less to both the taker and the taken. At the same time, every confiscation is a disincentive to future production. When our earnings are taken away, we have less reason to earn, and we will do less tomorrow.

The worst part of the whole tax-thy-neighbor system is that it is so addictive—it feeds on itself. When so much of our money is taxed away, we feel cheated and lose all our moral qualms about getting to the trough ourselves, one way or another, to get it back. That's only fair, isn't it? No, it isn't. All we are doing is resorting to the same means that cheated us in the first place and we are giving overweening government its strongest hold on us.

A Brighter Road Ahead

There is a brighter road ahead, though, as evidenced by the fall of communism in Eastern Europe and the former Soviet Union. Against seemingly impossible odds, country after country has thrown off its communist yoke. In the Christmas season of 1989, we all watched a very special celebration in Berlin, and we knew the impossible dream had come true. East and West Berliners, reunited after decades, hugged, laughed, poured champagne, wept, and defiantly danced on that monument to barbarity that had divided them, the Berlin Wall. Uncounted millions wept and laughed with them, and church bells rang the world over. Here, for all humanity to see, was the symbolic reunion of long-divided Europe and of the world, in freedom.

Here, too, all saw that communism was no longer a potent idea contending for the minds and hearts of men. It was just one more instrument of power, naked power of men over men, such as we have seen countless times before in history. Its last pretensions as an idealistic moral philosophy collapsed as its borders were broken. The crimes it had so long concealed were laid bare; it lay in the destruction and reek of its own works, economically exhausted and spiritually destitute.

To the inquiring souls among the younger generation, communism must seem like some evil, forgotten sect whose incantations and chants were like witch doctors shaking bones. (Whatever did they mean by "dialectical materialism" or "the theory of surplus value"?) Those of us who have been through more of the struggle may find these events more like awakening in surprise and immense relief as an awful nightmare ends.

In Prague, Warsaw, Budapest, and even in Moscow, the celebration of the triumph of capitalism that has been so conspicuously lacking in the West has been loud, exuberant, and unrestrained. Obviously, we take our market economy too much for granted. It has been more admired, and at times better understood, where it was absent and where the brunt of a coercive system was felt everyday. In fact, there was a poll taken among ordinary Moscow citizens with this question: "Which system do you think is superior to the other, capitalism or socialism?" The response was: capitalism, 51 percent; socialism, 32 percent. I'm glad they didn't poll Harvard.

In this vein, my favorite story is one about the huge Institute of Marxism-Leninism in Czechoslovakia. It was disbanded as soon as the communist rulers were tossed out, except for its Department of Bourgeois Economics, which had been set up to study our ideas in order to use them against us. The staff in this department had secretly become capitalists through reading the works of Ludwig von Mises, F. A. von Hayek, Milton Friedman and other defenders of the free market. Said the new Czech finance minister, "The world is run by human action, not by human design"—a plain reference to Mises' masterwork, *Human Action.* (One of Hillsdale College's proudest possessions is the personal library of Ludwig von Mises, who left the entire annotated collection of his beloved books to Hillsdale College, which he described as "that educational institution which most strongly represents the free market ideas to which I have given my life.")

Events in the postcommunist world—and here I am not even talking about political events or the violence that has erupted in Bosnia, Azerbaijan, and elsewhere—are still swirling and changing too rapidly to foresee how they will end. It is not going to be easy for citizens of the new republics to rebuild their decimated economies or to learn the ways of entrepreneurial capitalism after decades of suppression. But they have three things going for them that give great hope. First, they have their churches back—churches that were, in fact, highly instrumental in the downfall of communist rule, by their teaching and moral leadership. Second, they know at least the theory of free markets—I think they could teach us a thing or two—and they certainly have experience in how not to run an economy. Third, in large measure, they have their freedom back. Freedom is what makes everything work. We don't know quite how, because we can't predict what free men and women will do, but we can be confident that they will find ways to make things work.

Something else I've noticed that hasn't been mentioned anywhere is how direct and blunt the new leaders in Eastern Europe and Russia are. They talk as if they had long been truth-starved, as indeed they were, and use none of the evasions or nuances of politicians. And they tell us incredible things. All this time, they say, they were cheated. Communism was a hoax. It wasted their hard labor. It left them with nothing. Worse, it made war on their spirit and left behind "a decayed moral environment," in the words of Czech President Vaclav Havel.

Back in 1984, an East German girl, wise beyond her years, sadly told a visitor from the West: "It doesn't make any difference what we become when we grow up. We will still always be treated like children." She was saying, like Havel, that the very fulfillment of life through adult responsibility and moral choice was impossible under communist suppression. Others—God bless the human spirit that can laugh even in the worst of times—have said the same thing with jokes. Here is the wry assessment of an East German on "the six miracles of socialism":

- There is no unemployment, but no one works.
- No one works, but everyone gets paid.

- Everyone gets paid, but there is nothing to buy.
- No one can buy anything, but everyone owns everything.
- Everyone owns everything, but no one is satisfied.
- No one is satisfied, but 99 percent of the people voted for the system.

What Free Men Know

For nearly a century, the Left in this country has claimed that socialism, whether represented by Soviet-style communism or European-style socialism, is morally superior to our market-based capitalist system. They have criticized every aspect of America, all the while chanting their chants and rattling their bones. They have compared our "failures," real and imagined, with their utopian pipe dreams.

Through the testimony of those forced to live under communism and socialism, we know that the truth is exactly the opposite of all the promises. In the former Soviet Union, in the name of "equality" and "economic justice," the Party bosses gave themselves a cut of the wealth one hundred to one thousand times greater than that of the masses. They created a ruling class, the *nomenklatura,* more autocratic and exploitative than the tsars. In a system much like apartheid, except far more virulent, they reserved for themselves all the top jobs, the best education, the best medical care, and up to 100 percent of the quality goods sold in special stores that only they could patronize.

So shamelessly did the *nomenklatura* bleed workers that, by some of their own calculations, it was estimated that 86.5 percent of the Soviet population were dirt poor. Many did not have running water or electricity. Only 11.2 percent of the population could be called middle class. That left just 2.3 percent with virtually all the power and privilege; and among these was a "super-elite" of about 400,000 people who alone had access to such luxuries as the system was able to import. The promises were all frauds. "Power to the people" turned out to be totalitarian power in the hands of a tiny, highly privileged ruling class. "Economic justice" turned out to be rank exploitation.

Recent years have been bad for the *nomenklatura* and good for the people. The cause of freedom has blossomed not only in Eastern Europe and Russia but around the world. Today, for the first time in history, a greater number of the world's people are free than are not. Many more enjoy some limited freedoms, and free nations outnumber the unfree.

Free men know what tyrants never learn, that the ultimate economic resource is the mind and energy of a free person. Only from a free mind comes the direction of all productivity and the innovation that is tomorrow's prosperity. It is said that we now live in an information economy. This is true enough, but it is not the whole picture. Add to it an unprecedented mobility for the movement of economic resources—assets as well as data. Thought and money can and do travel almost anywhere in a split second, too fast for the plodding state to catch up. It is this mobility and versatility that gives individuals the upper hand at last. There is no turning back.

The growing power of the global marketplace is bringing this fact home everywhere. Its power has exposed the weaknesses of socialism and communism and has helped tear down the Iron Curtain. Its power is fundamentally moral and as such deserves all the moral support we can give it. The message of the postcommunist newcomers to the marketplace is directed toward every would-be tyrant: "We are not things to be used by you, but free people with inalienable rights. In the market, it does not matter how we came into the world but what we make of ourselves. We join in cooperative effort for the good of all. If you interfere, you harm all people. If you oppress us, you will lose all that we have to offer and become poor. Throw away your chains and your barbed wire; they are useless now."

Tomorrow's Agenda

As I said at the outset, communism is dying, but we need no more than the unrepentant Left to remind us that the war of ideas is not over. It may even grow more intense. The rejection of communism leaves a vacuum that other "isms" and ideologies will rush to fill. Certainly among them will be milder forms of socialism that build the power of the state. It is the business of all who stand for individual rights in a civilized order to refute these efforts and make our own ideas heard. The answer to bad ideas is good ideas. Let us never forget that the war of ideas is a real war, with real casualties should we fail.

One cannot predict the politics and perils of tomorrow exactly, but the enemies of the moral order change little. We know them. We can in some measure anticipate their assaults by their beliefs and goals and plan our own strategy accordingly. The enemy, as ever, will be the exploiters, the wielders of power and privilege. They will take positions against the traditional and the normal, against home and family, against distinction between man and woman, against human nature itself: positions which, on analysis, will treat people as mere conveniences to somebody's plans, not as individuals of infinite worth. Whatever they seek, they will be armed with ideological formulas and warped words. Above all, they will try to force their schemes on us, using the power of government.

Such resort to government "solutions" always seems to me a giveaway that something wrong or dishonest is involved. In freedom, persuasion—not coercion—is the way to get one's ideas across, and the only way. Imposing them by law denies to others their liberty, their dignity, their right to their own opinions. It is, in fact, an act of contempt toward them and an act of pride in oneself—a claim to know better than we what is best for us. In the view of Nobel laureate F. A. von Hayek, this is the "fatal conceit." In the Judeo-Christian view, it is sin. Deep down, it implies a false, secularist view of life that throughout this century has been at war with Western, and especially American, ideals. It is precisely the kind of thinking that has collapsed due to hard experience in Eastern Europe and Russia; but it is still rampant here. We need not know the whys and wherefores of a given statist scheme to realize that it serves bent thinking and bad purposes. It will, of course, be made to sound good, as if it were correcting injustice instead of creating it, or helping the needy instead of making them dependent and helpless. It will, of course, have the support of all the familiar "opinion makers" in the academy, the media and the Washington bureaucracy. But it is going to cost us dearly, not only in taxes and liberty but in moral values.

Certainly in the coming years we will have to deal with liberalism, a set of once-noble ideas that sold its soul to statism decades ago and now grows more decadent every day. It remains strong, but as a reflex. Tap any liberal with a rubber hammer, and an informed person can predict where the knee will jerk. The reflex the Left constantly encourages is: Uncle Sam is there to do what individuals can't or won't accomplish on their own. If we agree with this reflex, we forget the basic facts of life. Government can't do anything for us without first taking from us the means to do it. Government's only tool is force, and force is usually the worst possible tool to apply in social matters. Neither must we forget that we ourselves, as free men and women, are the doers, builders, and producers. Running to Uncle Sam with our problems only takes away from our own freedom and resourcefulness.

We have, I'm afraid, lost our fear of big government, and

we had better regain it soon. America is not immune to suffocation by an Old World-type state, any more than Eastern Europe or Russia has been. Our survival is at stake. We are seeing momentous change around us, but cannot be sure where it will take us. Will a springtime of liberty bloom into a full summer of peace? Or will our hopes collapse before some new peril? Surely it is up to us to create the right tomorrow for our children by taking charge today. There has never been a generation in the history of the world that has had such an enormous opportunity to make a clear choice and to have such a strong hand in implementing that choice. We can play our part in shaping the world now emerging, or we can stand aside and be overrun. The other side is working against us. We have to be better. We have to lead with the right ideas.

Ideas, not armies, rule the world. We believed too easily that tanks, barbed wire, secret police, and instruments of thought control and totalitarian power were decisive and that slaves could never be free. The events of the last several years have proved us wrong. It was false belief, not barbed wire, that enslaved. In the end, the wire was cut and the Iron Curtain broken by simple human choice, not arms. Those who had been trapped behind the barricades said, "Enough!" and were freed.

Vitaly A. Naishul

Perspectives on Economic Reform in Russia

I. Introduction

The Situation in Russia in the Early 1990s

During the early 1990s, Russia was going through yet another difficult stage in the transition from a socialist to a free society. The economic reforms the government had instituted up until this time only partially justified the great hopes—and risks—with which the movement towards liberalization had begun. On the one hand, the people as a whole had adapted to the new economic situation rather easily. They did not protest against reforms and, indeed, they appeared to welcome them. It seems that during February through May of 1993, they began to respect the authorities in power, at least as much as was possible when the government was so unprecedentedly weak. On the other hand, there were very few new opportunities in the economy compared with the high market-oriented expectations so many citizens shared.

This edited essay is based on a report written by V.A. Naishul, prepared in cooperation with V.V. Agroskin, V.F. Chesnokova, V.L. Kagansky, S.G. Kordonsky, G.V. Lebedev, A.I. Levenchuk, B.M. Lvin, S. Yu. Pavlenko, and G.G. Sapov.

The same government that had made the first decisive moves in the direction of liberalization of the economy in 1990-92, suddenly stopped in 1993. True, it was still continuing to pursue a few sound measures, like freeing up energy prices, but it had backed away from major reforms, and it was still relying out of habit on administrative, i.e., bureaucratic, methods to find the solutions to economic problems.

Regarding its initial price reforms, the government did deserve credit for strengthening the role of finance in Russia, which has always been a centralized resource. But since then, it has succumbed to economic and political pressure exerted by: (1) a variety of powerful interest groups; (2) its own considerations of the efficiency and merits of different industries; and (3) its own officials' self-interest and ambition. Consequently, the government has abandoned its earlier commitment to price reforms and is currently using financial leverage, as well as all the attendant privileges and licenses, with the same or perhaps even greater arbitrariness than Brezhnev's central agencies used to allocate planned physical resources.

But many people failed to comprehend the true nature of this situation. As Elena Bonner put it at the time, *perestroika* and the forces of liberalization were giving way to democratic and economic stagnation. Many unresolved problems intensified public tension in 1993 and made the political process ineffective. The paternalistic state was supposedly no more, and people were supposedly free, but so many vestiges of socialism remained that they had no real opportunity to take responsibility for governing, to care for themselves and their families, or to launch new ventures in the marketplace.

The reform government led by Gaidar made two monumental mistakes which were to lead to crisis. First, it attempted to impose a monetary system alien to the national economy of Russia. Second, it gave no real support to the liberalization of the state sector, and its rigidities in effect broke the threads on the nuts and bolts of a tight monetary policy. Everyone who was familiar with the nature of central planning bodies knew of the problems attached to reform: the difficulty of ensuring efficient production and the equitable distribution of goods and services; the temptation to give in to the requests of needy friends and past allies; and the corruption of easily bribed officials. They also knew that it was easier for a heavily centralized and politicized banking system to simply issue more currency—a commodity that takes little effort or expense to produce—than to address actual economic reforms that, however sound, might be unpopular, demanding, or threatening to the system's own existence.

No less important is the fact that stabilization measures neglected the variety of exchange relations which existed before reforms. Some elements within retail trade and industry, as well as within the general population, had been used to monetized exchanges, but many had not, and this further contributed to the weakening of Russia's financial condition and the value of the ruble.

The government hesitated to follow the tough but sensible monetary policies of classical liberalism devised by Ludwig von Mises, F.A. Hayek, and other defenders of laissez faire economics. Such policies treat money as a market commodity, promoting current exchanges and future transactions, but also support nonmonetary exchanges, ranging from automobile tires and jeans to rubles and dollars. They also support free competition between currencies and all other forms of exchange.

The Russian government could not introduce classical liberal economic policies while trying as it did (and still does) to simultaneously preserve the legitimacy of hierarchical, bureaucratic relations and old socialist regulations. Except for the deregulation of the street retail trade conducted under the influence of the Polish experience, the government has not taken any steps to provide serious liberalization of trade or any productive activities. Moreover, analysis of Gaidar's and other key officials' actions in the early 1990s shows that government itself has become a major source of economic restrictions. Many measures such as heavy taxation contribute to the inflexibility of the economy by driving business activities into the black market. This in turn creates even greater obstacles to the formation of legal market institutions.

II. Prerequisites of Classical Liberal Economic Policy

Withering of the State

The aim of the former socialist system of economic management was to eradicate free action in the marketplace and substitute "scientific," or "planned," administrative production and distribution. However, the system appeared to be workable only under certain narrow conditions; substantial changes in these conditions in the 1950s led to the spontaneous transformation of the administrative command system into an adminstrative or bureaucratic market. Ironically, the trade that was eliminated outside the state sector started to develop *within it.* The flourishing of this administrative trade led in turn to rapid formation of administrative bodies' autonomous economic rights—a development which came to be known as *"veodomstvenost,"* or, "departmentalism."

The decline of the socialist regime in the late 1980s and early 1990s, intensified by *perestroika* and especially by the withdrawal of the Communist Party (which had been used to integrate all power structures), led to the further autonomization of state bodies and the growth of their freedom to make transactions and to develop extra business activities and sources of revenues. To a very large extent, bureaucratic trade was then replaced by barter trade and regular trade, and former state departments were essentially transformed into commercial agencies that pursued their own economic interests.

In this context, Russia is now facing two vital and mutually connected tasks. The first is to complete the process of commercialization of state agencies and relieve them from bureaucratic relations (a separation, if you will, of the economy from the state). The second is to establish an effective, nontrading government that will protect rather than restrict private property and contractual rights (a separation of the state from the economy).

Structural Policy

According to many scientists and, notably, the "scientific school" headed by Dr. Y.V. Yaremenko, the economy of Russia is full of structural inequities and is far from being in the homogenous condition necessary for the efficient establishment and functioning of a market economy. Two fundamentally different economic approaches, therefore, are vying for the support of the people and the government. One is the traditional structural approach, which holds that it is expedient to divide the economy into several more or less homogenous sectors and establish for each a specific set of "game rules" governing taxation, exchange rates, economic privileges, etc. This approach assumes that the state has enough organizational potential to draw borders between sectors and execute proper control.

According to the classical liberal approach, the free market alone, without interference, leaves sufficient room for structural differences. Equity problems tend to be short-lived and are efficiently remedied by competition—unless, of course, the state imposes restrictions on economic activities. A recent example of intervention occurred in 1992, when a deep disparity existed between monetary and nonmonetary, or accounting rubles, so their informal exchange rate was two to one. In the past, the structuralist approach was to maintain strict control over all exchanges (the classical liberal approach held, in contrast, that it was beneficial to accept a free exchange rate between the two types.) In practice, however, disparities were simply ignored by the government because it established an artificial exchange rate of 1:1, which caused a cash crunch in the beginning and high inflation afterwards.

It seems that the weakness of the modern Russian state (to be exact, its practical absence, so that all laws are open to challenge or barter) will no longer allow it to exercise a structuralist policy. Under the pretext of exercising it, however, the government has allowed corruption to reign. The strongest interest groups, including those within state agencies, have engaged in the dishonest distribution of favors and privileges. Only liberalization based on classical liberal principles can salvage the government's reform campaign and the Russian economy.

The Constitution of Society

There are at least two important premises that make a classical liberal solution to Russia's problems feasible. First, is the premise that the effective functioning of the old administrative system depended on the standardization and uniformity of the objects of management. A high degree of homogenity was artificially achieved because the structuralist approach reigned for over fifty years. According to Dr. Boris M. Lvin, this eliminated the danger of serious conflicts and was actually a prerequisite of the formation of a liberal society.

Second, long-term prohibition of independent activities intensified development of internal ties, practically hidden from state interference. The existence of a large, informal, nonstate network, through which the greater part of consumer needs was and still is being realized, makes society ready and able to self-organize and preserve stability while the state withers. This means that state control can be withdrawn from most spheres of life without risking destabilization.

The Tasks of the Central Government

The central authorities can influence spontaneous reforms, depriving the old bureaucratic relations of legitimacy, thus liberalizing the economy. The central government is too weak to construct either a new society or a new state. However, it has the right to legitimize the state hierarchical relations and therefore can shape the development of a new state system.

III. Liberal Reform

Institutional Liberalization

The first step of classical liberal reform, made by the government's liberalization of prices, meant de facto termination of central authorities' legal support of the previous mutual obligations (between the population on the one hand and the retail trade of the state and state enterprises on the other) in relation to prices and renumeration of labor. It is now necessary to complete this process through liberalization of relations between organizations. That means termination of central authorities' support of mutual bureaucratic claims of various state departments (including state enterprises).

This step may be characterized as an *institutional liberalization*. The central government can proclaim that it will no longer support subordination of all former state departments, except for an explicitly stipulated list. Institutional liberalization is the logical conclusion and the last point in the process of state departments' liberalization and will take several decades. Its completion will mean the culmination of market-oriented reform in the Russian economy.

Indeed, institutional liberalization means total privatization of practically all state property. After this step, only local intergroup struggles for redistribution of property can emerge. Most of these conflicts will be settled informally. Only in rare cases will court intervention be necessary, and customary law and existing legal norms will be sufficient to decide the division of common property. Institutional liberalization also means total deregulation, because it presumes termination of subordination to almost all former state regulatory offices. (From the libertarian perspective, of course, institutional liberalization could make the economy even more liquid if it would be possible to extend it to revenue services and abolish compulsory taxation.)

Limits of the State

What should be the functions of the new Russian state? As the experience of the world has shown, practically all public goods, such as communications, education, medical services, and even the monetary system, can be privatized. Some spontaneous processes in our country are going in this very direction. However, there are functions that cannot be alienated from the state if its citizens desire permanent internal peace. First among these functions is the conduct of foreign policy. Second, the state must guarantee that every conflict in society that cannot settled on the basis of mutual agreement or compromise will be resolved through the rule of law. (At the same time in most cases nonstate institutions may be used to carry out legal decisions. For instance, a criminal investigation may be carried out by a private agency; private security firms may also be used to maintain order and police the streets.)

Privatization of Russia's Debts

Institutional liberalization will also lead to the abolition of almost all state assets. This means that the remaining state debts will put a heavy tax burden on the emerging market economy. Besides, even greater earnings will be lost as a result of strict control exercised by tax authorities in order to collect more revenues. The internal state pension debt to older citizens is the biggest single state liability. The amount of the debt in world prices greatly exceeds Russia's foreign debt and comprises more than $500 billion. Apparently, the pension debt can be efficiently privatized by way of transferring both land rights and pension liabilities (in the form of annuities) to local private funds. It is also possible to work out ways of privatizing all other state debts.

Taxation

Privatization of state debts, the withdrawal of the state from the economy, and military reform will allow for a sharp reduction of state expenditures to within several percentage points of the GNP. The cuts will encourage lower taxes as well as more revenue-producing economic activity and less tax evasion. Tax revenues will actually rise. Currently, a number of economists in Russia are working on the idea of extending institutional liberalization to the abolition of most compulsory taxes. This, goal, though seemingly over-optimistic, is not beyond the realm of possibility. It would certainly facilitate the opening of more global economic activity. Revenue for necessary state operations would come from other sources and from certain "social mechanisms" that would help citizens finance minimal state expenditures.

Reform of the Monetary System

One of the main results of institutional liberalization would be changes in the monetary system. Practically speaking this entails the following: (1) the Central Bank of Russia will become the only commercial bank that will have its own banknotes denominated in the rubles of current issue. These rubles will compete with foreign currencies and probably with the banknotes of other commercial banks; (2) each commercial bank will be able to quote deposit money of other banks so that excessive issue will be curbed by a falling exchange rate; and (3) banking activity in Russia will be opened to foreign banks that will establish modern banking technology and standards of credibility and service.

So, Russia will develop a free banking system with competitive currencies analogous to the system that existed in Western countries before the establishment of centralized banking. Under this system, there will be no state body responsible for the amount of money in circulation, and thus no inflation, inevitable in other cases.

Aaron Wildavsky

Chronicle of a Collapse Foretold: How Marx Predicted the Demise of Communism (Although He called It "Capitalism")

Communism has been collapsing for a long time. For many years, it has been difficult to watch the Soviet world of "real socialism" without experiencing an eerie sense of *deja vu*. Consider Poland, in many ways the most "developed" among communist political economies (CPEs), if only because the symptoms of its disease had advanced furthest. For first-time visitors in the 1970s and 1980s, the dinginess of the streets, the cramped housing, the lack of palatable food in shops, the sallow complexions of the inhabitants, the smoke-filled skies all looked familiar. The more literary-minded may have thought of *Bleak House:* There was indeed a more than passing resemblance between the contemporary reality of cities like Warsaw or Moscow and Charles Dickens's vivid descriptions of London a century earlier. Had they talked to the inhabitants, though, the Western visitors would have heard bitter denunciations of exploitation and unmistakable expressions of alienation; they would have been told of an immense gap between the people and

---

This essay was coauthored by John Clark, a graduate student at the University of California-Berkeley.

the ruling class, between "us" and "them." The sense of *deja vu* experienced in real socialist countries, in other words, would have evoked memories of the scathing attacks upon capitalism written by the man upon whose thought these societies were supposedly based: Karl Marx.

The collapse of communist regime after regime in 1989—as well as the even more rapid disintegration of the erstwhile Soviet Union following the downfall of the August coup—served to heighten the sense of having seen it all before.[1] It was not only a matter of Marx's picture of capitalism fitting real socialism better than contemporary capitalism: his predictions about the fate of capitalism really did come to pass—only they were fulfilled in communist rather than capitalist countries. Again, consider Poland. By the mid-1970s, it was apparent that Poland was experiencing the same kinds of economic crises and collapse Marx analyzed in detail in *Capital*. The year 1980 witnessed the birth of Solidarity, seen by some as the first clear case of the workers' revolution foretold a century before by Marx. The problem for Marxists in the region was that the workers rose up against communism, not in favor of it.

Others have remarked on the similarity between Marx's predictions for capitalism and the fate of the social order his descendants constructed.[2] But whereas most have only noted the irony, perhaps gloating a bit, it seems important to take the similarity far more seriously. Marx, in his analyses of and predictions about capitalism, really does have something to tell us about the collapse of communism. The close fit between Marx's predictions for capitalism and the actual experience of communism is much more than coincidental. However unintentional the fit may be, Marx's analyses of the anticipated collapse of capitalism do in fact go far in explaining both the long-term decay and the more recent collapse of Soviet-style communist political economies (CPEs).

Real socialism suffers from a chronic condition Adam

Michnik calls the "brittleness of totalitarian stability."[3] On the one hand, these systems managed to persist for decades in Eastern Europe, for even longer in the U.S.S.R., without undergoing significant institutional change. They persisted without reform in spite of disastrous economic performance, in spite of the world's highest levels of pollution and environmental damage, in spite of society's festering and sullen mistrust of government, in spite of wide-spread corruption by the rulers and the even more wide-spread criminalization of a populace forced to break the law every day simply to get by. CPEs persisted in spite of periodic and, in many cases, sincere attempts by their rulers to rectify the most egregious of the system's many flaws. This is a remarkable record of stability-cum-inertia. On the other hand, when they collapsed, they did so with a suddenness and a finality that was breathtaking. A challenge for social scientists today is to explain the peculiarly stable yet fragile rigidity that preceded the eventual collapse of real socialism.

For this reason, bringing Marx into the discussion about the fall of communism is essential. This is the way, or perhaps one way, Marx thought capitalism would collapse. It would be unable to make the systemic reforms that could ensure its continued survival, continuing blindly to its doom. Set aside for a moment the question of his responsibility for the outrage of real socialism in the first place. Marx devoted a lifetime of intense thought and research to the study of revolution. More than almost anyone else, he sought to unravel questions about how an unjust and unpopular social system can hold itself together for a time, then crumble, then be replaced by forces that it had created within itself. While the fact that he was wrong about where and when revolution would take place is important, it should not blind us to the valuable insights in his analyses.

For the Marxist, it is an appalling realization that the societies established in his name (perhaps "in their name" might also be accurate) in fact embodied virtually everything the master detested about capitalism. Oscar Wilde noted how often we kill the thing we love. But Marx's ideological descendants have failed to notice how much they have created the very thing they hate.

Problems Predicting and What to Do About Them

It is important to emphasize that we do not mean to let capitalists off the hook. No one can deny that market economies have serious flaws. As the heady flush of triumph after the events of 1989, East Europeans are realizing this more and more with each passing day. What we are arguing is that one particularly powerful indictment of capitalism—Karl Marx's—applies to modern communist political economies much better than it does to comparable capitalist democracies. We don't have to compare the United States and the late Soviet Union to prove this point. Let's stick with countries that were at similar points of economic development at the end of World War II, when communism was introduced on a wide scale. Contrast North and South Korea, or what once was East and West Germany, or Poland and Spain, or Czechoslovakia and Austria, or Bulgaria and Portugal. Choose virtually any index of quality of life, and you'll see the former countries come off worse than the latter.[4]

In a fundamental way, this means taking Marx more seriously than do many Marxists. Marx hated capitalism with a passion, but in formulating his critique he did not include just any grievance. In fact, he was quite contemptuous of rival critics of capitalism—young Hegelians, anarchists, socialists—who condemned capitalism's immorality, injustice, inequality, etc., without, in his opinion, thinking through the bases of their hostility of capitalism. Marx's critique was of an entire social order, not just of particular parts of it. As it became clear to Marxists (even though they had a difficult time admitting it) that real-life capitalism was bearing less and less resemblance to the capitalism of Marx's critique, they responded in one of two ways: some tenaciously held onto the totality of Marx's critique, losing almost any connection to the outside world; others sought to develop some particular aspect of Marx's criticisms of capitalism, ignoring the fact that Marx was talking about an entire, cohesive system.

It has only been recently that analysts have again begun paying serious attention to exactly what is entailed by Marx's critical project. N. Scott Arnold's excellent book, *Marx's Radical Critique of Capitalism,* not only lays out the interconnections of Marx's critique, but shows clearly where it fails: many of Marx's particular criticisms are not well-founded; he fails to articulate a satisfactory normative theory; he fails to spell out the institutions of a feasible and stable postcapitalist society; moreover, the communism he does spell out, insofar as it is based on central planning, is likely when put into practice to be more exploitive than capitalism in practice.[5] Arnold is correct about Marx's failed radical critique of capitalism, but Marx's radical critique of *communism*—a social order he never witnessed, but that is foreshadowed by his model of capitalism—is quite valid.

Some Marxists have taken seriously the challenge of applying Marx's critique of capitalism to Soviet-style socialism. State capitalist theorists, who claim the communism went wrong because the party-state acts as a monopoly capitalist, find a common culprit responsible for the exploitation and alienation they believe is experienced on both sides of the Iron Curtain—social inequality.[6] This approach to communism suffers from a deep and obvious conceptual problem. "In what sense," ask Feher, Heller, and Markus,

> can societies characterized by an absence of private property in the means of production, by the far-reaching reduction of market mechanisms (bordering on

liquidation), by the dissolution of the institutional separation between economy and state and by a general tendency to abolish the distinction between the public-political sphere and that of civil society—in what sense can such societies be called capitalist at all?[7]

Marxists, after all, are the ones who define capitalism as possessing these features. Isn't it changing the rules in the middle of the game to say that just because they don't like a social system and just because there are obvious inequities and injustices it must be capitalist? The question raised above points us toward an answer. In what sense are these countries capitalist? In the sense that Marxists conceive of capitalism. Ruling communist parties do not behave like the capitalists we see in reality; they behave exactly like the capitalists Marx describes.

In this sense, we can answer one of the major charges addressed by orthodox Marxists against their comrades who accused the U.S.S.R. of being "state capitalist." Some of Marx's most important concepts seem to be almost impossible to use in analyzing communist countries. "Surplus value" and the "labor theory of value" in general headed the list. Marxists have spent much time and energy arguing with one another about whether a social order restricting and repressing the market, as Soviet-type economies do, actually product surplus value. It is not necessary to note, however, that insofar as such concepts depend on the by-now-discredited labor theory of value, an increasing number of Marxist political economists believe they do not apply to capitalism. It seems more useful to view all factors of production, including capital and management, as at least potentially having value. What is interesting is that while surplus value has no particular explanatory usefulness or empirical content in capitalism, it can be directly applied to communism. This is because in communist economies forced-investment is secured by depressing consumption, providing for the owners of "political capital" (the political elite of the Party) a surplus creamed off to provide unsustainable levels of investment.

Rather than quibbling over whether or not surplus value exists in communist economies, look at the function a concept like surplus value fills within Marxist thought. Surplus value refers (in essence) to the profits capitalists can reap from the "unpaid" labor time of their employees. This unpaid surplus can be increased in two ways. It can be extended extensively by increasing "absolute surplus value." In other words, capitalists can increase the amount of labor their employees perform by forcing more work out of them through greater labor discipline, or by forcing them to stay on the job for longer hours at the same daily wage rate. Surplus value can also be increased intensively, through increasing "relative surplus value" by replacing "living labor" with "dead labor," Marx's evocative way of talking about mechanizing production. Fewer hours of work performed by the proletariat yields greater profits when the work is made more productive by machinery. The individual capitalist benefits from the increase of relative surplus value because he gets more goods and services while having to pay fewer workers. The capitalist class as a whole benefits (for a short time) because the workers made redundant by technological improvement form a reserve army of the unemployed that drives down the average wage rate.

Marx intended the concept of surplus value to show that capitalist economic growth is an unavoidably conflict-ridden and self-destructive process, conflict-ridden because gains for the capitalist come only at a cost to workers, and self-destructive because increasing surplus value undermines the bases of the economic system. Workers are destroyed when absolute surplus value is increased. Even if a worker does manage to win benefits for himself, they come at the expense of his class as a whole. "To clamor for equal or even more equitable retribution on the basis of the wage system,"

Marx says, "is the same as to clamor for freedom on the basis of the slavery system."[8] What is worse, the capitalist is constantly clawing to win these gains back. The dog-eat-dog struggle depicted, however, is quite an accurate picture of the labor process in real socialist countries.

Here is where it is important to pay attention to Marxists' predictions as well as their condemnations. State capitalist theorists predicted that the economic and political performance of both Western market capitalism and Eastern state capitalism would decline. They anticipated that crises in both systems would recur and worsen. They hoped that a proletarian revolution would take place, institutionalizing a new, improved, and genuinely socialist economy. So far, however, only one of the systems has collapsed.

Predictions are hard, however, whether they are about the future or about the past. No matter if they are antagonistic or sympathetic to Marxism, anyone who has tried to extract falsifiable predictions from the corpus of Marx's writings will tell you that it is not an easy task. Some Marxists even act as though Marx did not make predictions. He does. Fred Gottheil organizes 176 of Marx's predictions in testable forms. (Unfortunately, Gottheil does not test the predictions he identifies.)[9] Marx was engaged in the process of creating, almost *ab ovo*, a vocabulary and methodology for analyzing political economy and history, so it is not surprising that not everything he wrote is consistent. Because "bourgeois" (or more accurately, non-Marxist) social scientists have rejected most of Marx's fundamental tenets, his basic concepts, and the methods he thinks ought to govern science, it also is not surprising that usable statistics framed in Marxism terms are hard to come by.

Matters are made worse by what can only be described as Marxists' cavalier attitude about testing the predictions Marx does make.[10] On the very first page of *History and Class Consciousness*, which during the 1960s and 1970s was perhaps the most influential Marxian work of philosophy,

Georg Lukacs says:

> Let us assume for the sake of argument that recent research disproved once and for all every one of Marx's individual theses. Even if this were to be proved, every serious "orthodox" Marxist would still be able to accept all such modern findings without reservation and hence dismiss all of Marx's theses *in toto*—without having to renounce his orthodoxy for a single moment.[11]

In saying this, Lukacs is at odds with his teacher, Max Weber, who says: "Scientific works ... will be surpassed scientifically—let that be repeated—for it is our common fate and, more, our common goal. We cannot work without hoping that others will advance further than we have."[12] A failed prediction is part of science, a reason in some cases to revise the theory from which the prediction was derived. Unfortunately, Lukacs and many others have blithely proceeded with their critiques as though it does not matter whether or not specific predictions come true or not. And all too many Marxists dismiss a preoccupation with formulating and testing hypotheses as "positivistic" and hence bourgeois. Waving Marx's Eleventh Thesis on Feuerbach over their heads, they proclaim that the point of science is to change the world, not to explain it. Far easier than reformulating Marx's theory—or even worse, admitting it to be wrong in some fundamental respect—is simply citing a contrary statement or two from Marx's four decades of writing, saying he was correct after all and, if necessary, dismissing the supposed refutation of the master as arising from improper motives (as though the intentions of analysis relate at all to its validity). That is why we do not receive much help from his adherents in applying Marx's predictions to the fate of real socialism.

Marxists are not the only ones to experience problems falsifying their predictions. Modern philosophers of science are divided over the role that falsification does and ought to play in science.[13] A rational, even somewhat noble, view of science is advanced by those, like Karl Popper and Imre Lakatos, who see science as a process of advancement based on the formulation and disproof of testable hypotheses.[14] More true to the facts of actual research is Thomas Kuhn's debunking view of scientists defending research paradigms in which they have a stake through the use of qualifying conditions that protect their hypotheses from being disproved.[15] Insofar as Marxists have a theoretic "paradigm" they have been seeking to develop, this might explain their reluctance to test, and possibly have to reject, Marx's predictions. The problem, not surprisingly, is that it is possible to lose contact with the real world, to become so committed to introducing qualifying condition after qualifying condition that the theory becomes senseless.

Trying to prove a negative—that a theory has no applicability—is difficult. It certainly is unlikely to convince those committed to defending the theory. That is why it is illuminating to choose a different form of refutation: It is not necessary to show that Marx's predictions have *no* applicability to modern capitalist countries; rather, it is necessary only to demonstrate how well his predictions fit the evidence of communist nations. Plainly, if Marx's description of capitalism fits twentieth-century communism better than contemporary capitalism and if his predictions of capitalism's fate have come to pass for communism rather than capitalism, then Marxists have a problem applying the words of the master to the capitalist world today.

Marx's Mechanisms of Capitalism at Work in Communism

The falling rate of profit seems like the most promising mechanism underlying making and testing predictions about capitalism and communism. Marx calls this the centerpiece of his economic theory, one that is "in every respect the most important law in modern political economy, and the most essential for understanding the most difficult relations."[16] Although they may be wrong, economists since Adam Smith have believed that profits would fall over time, but Marx argues that they did not see the true cause. Ricardo and Malthus, for instance, think the declining rate of profit results from diminishing agricultural productivity—as Marx says, Ricardo flees "from economics to seek refuge in organic chemistry."[17] In other words, they treat falling profit as something natural, and thus unavoidable. Technological progress, they say, might postpone matters, but only temporarily. Marx prides himself on the discovery that the falling rate of profit is socially conditioned, not natural. It is a consequence of the way economic life is organized in capitalism. As Simon Clarke says correctly about the Marxian view of capitalism's inherent drive toward crisis,

> for Marx, as for the whole of the orthodox Marxist tradition, the source of crisis lay in the contradiction between the capitalist tendency to develop the productive forces without limit, on the one hand, and the tendency to restrict the consumption power of the mass of the population, on the other.... The fall in the rate of profit is not a cause of the crisis; it is its expression, the expression of the failure of capital to realize the mass of surplus value which it has produced.[18]

Contrary to the classical economists, Marx thinks the rate of profit falls *because* of technological change, not because there is not enough technological development.[19]

Progress comes at a price in capitalism, a very high price indeed. New technology, Marx argues, can be adopted only at the cost of the bankrupting of those firms slower to innovate, imposing hardship on workers in these firms, who are now unemployed, as well as on the erstwhile owners of these firms, who may be forced into the working class. There is also the hardship of those workers in the surviving innovative firms who were made redundant because of the introduction of labor-saving technology. This, Marx feels, is one of the most glaring examples of the senseless inefficiency of capitalism: Capitalists must run as fast as they can just to stay alive, and even when they do stay alive it is the proletariat that bears the brunt of the sacrifices.

Although his followers cling to Marx's notion of the declining rate of profit, Marx himself is careful to qualify his predictions. He identifies several factors that might temporarily ameliorate the fall of the rate of profit: Employers can increase what Marx calls the rate of exploitation, or in layman's terms, can squeeze more work out of their employees; wages can be cut to less than subsistence levels; innovations might be capital- as well as labor-saving; and foreign trade can ease the pressure. Thus he refers to "the law of the tendency of the rate of profit to fall," as rather circuitous phrasing that expresses his reservations about anyone ever actually seeing the rate of profit fall at any given time. But all of these mitigating factors can be only temporary in staving off the inevitable fall.

Where does Marx go wrong? For one thing, he assumes that all technological improvements will result in making workers in the innovating firm redundant. He also assumes that a labor-saving innovation in one firm automatically results in decreasing demand for labor throughout the economy. Neither of these assumptions is well-founded. Many technical improvements lead to increased demand for workers both within the innovating enterprise and, more generally, throughout the economy. That the rate of profit in capitalism has not been falling—even as a secular tendency that can be temporarily slowed—can most easily be demonstrated by the fact that capitalist firms are profitable today. The considerable problems facing modern capitalist economies seem to result from factors quite different from Marx's notion of the falling rate of profit.

But he is quite right in his criticism of the classical economists who believed the tendency of the rate of profit to fall is natural and unavoidable. As Marx says, it really is socially conditioned and is a product of a particular social order. That social order is communism. The decline of the rate of profit is inexorable under real socialism, a fact that has long been known by specialists, and now is becoming obvious to everyone. The reasons are the same as Marx's in view of capitalism's declining profitability. Marx describes what has come to be known as extensive economic growth, growth that can be achieved only by bringing more and more resources—more labor, material, and investment—into the economy.

No one contests any more that CPEs were structurally unable to shift from extensive to intensive development. High rates of industrial growth were recorded in the early post-war years in Eastern Europe, when the industrial workforce was greatly increased by demobilized troops, peasants driven from their land, and women previously employed in the household. Investment resources were squeezed out by the collectivization of agriculture. By the late 1950s and 1960s, however, it was clear that it would no longer be possible to mobilize new investment for extensive development. The binge of borrowing from the West in the 1970s allowed the system to go on unchanged, but this only made the collapse harder when it came. Everyone agreed that if it was to survive in the absence of foreign credits, resources in the system would have to be used more efficiently. For decades, right up to the collapse of communism, economic reform was dedicated to shifting the system from extensive to intensive development. The reforms never worked: Resources never were used efficiently. In the end, even stagnation could be maintained only by pumping in more and more investment. Why this was so will be discussed in more detail below.

Once again, we can appeal to Simon Clarke's summary of Marx on capitalism for a concise statement of how the declining profitability of socialism led to crisis and collapse: Marx, he says, sees "the law of the tendency for the rate of profit to fall"

> as a secular law, the importance of which is that it intensifies the inherent contradictions of the capitalist mode of production, between the development of the forces of production expressed in the concentration and centralization of capital, and the relative pauperization of the mass of the population, expressed in the de-skilling of labor and the augmentation of the reserve army.[20]

Again, change the word "capitalist" to "communist," and he is entirely correct.

Bigger Is Better, Isn't It?

Marx derives many predictions about the structure of firms from capitalism's competition and the resulting falling rate of profit. The unceasing drive to improve the technology capitalist enterprises use in production leads to what he calls the concentration of capital, a growth in the size of firms. Firms become more productive as a result of innovation, he says, because innovation increases economies of scale and permits mass production. Constant technical change also leads to what he calls the *centralization of capital,* better known today as industrial concentration, the reduction of the number of independent firms within each sector of the economy brought about by the destruction and absorption of hitherto independent enterprises.[21] Competition means that smaller firms, which cannot mobilize as much capital, go bankrupt and have their assets taken over by bigger firms. "Competition ... always ends in the ruin of many small capitalists, whose capitals partly pass into the hands of their conquerors, and partly vanish completely."[22]

Has Marx's prediction—that capitalist enterprises will be bigger in average size and fewer in number—been borne out in capitalism? Yes and no. There is no shortage of large transnational corporations in today's capitalism. Moreover, after the mergers and leveraged buy-outs in the 1980s, there may well have been an increase in the number of very large conglomerates. But Marx clearly underestimated the survival and innovative potential of small enterprises. High tech firms are the best known examples: the cutting edge of innovation in the computer field, for instance, can be found in companies employing between twenty and a number people in Northern California, in the "M4 corridor" in England, in "Silicon Glen" in Scotland. Many studies show these firms "grow faster than the national average, create new products frequently, invest heavily in R & D, provide (probably) higher income returns to the founders and hire only or principally highly skilled labor."[23] Moreover, because they are more flexible than large corporations, small firms prove adept at exploiting niches and rapidly changing opportunities. It is no accident (to use a phrase Marxists are fond of) that the highest growth rates in Europe are posted in Northern Italy, and that the highest rates ever are found in Taiwan: The economies of both are based heavily on small firms.[24]

Here we see where Marx goes wrong for capitalism: He seems to have assumed, without any particular reason, that dynamism and bigness are necessarily correlated. But this is an assumption about industrial structure that is painfully appropriate in real socialism. Every communist economy in the world is dominated by a small number of gigantic firms that are grouped into truly enormous *kombinats* or industrial conglomerates. In most socialist countries, decision-makers at one time or another recognized that the concentration and centralization of industry is a major cause of their problems. That centralization and concentration of capital is truly a "law" of socialism (in the way that Marx saw it as a "law" of capitalist development) can be seen in the fact that every effort to reform the industrial structure through decentralization and deconcentration has failed abysmally.

Marx believed large capitalist firms would flourish at the expense of their smaller competitors because he assumed that only the giants would be able to invest in research and mobilize the large amounts of capital for technical development. Clearly, as shown by the experience of the last several decades in high-tech fields, that is not necessarily true in capitalism. It is true, however, that in CPEs only the large *kombinats* could introduce new technology. The reason why innovation was concentrated in the very biggest units was not that they were more imaginative or creative than smaller firms, but because communist political economies are particularly dependent on Western ideas. Innovation within CPEs was minimal for many reasons, especially because of the need managers felt to maintain production and not jeopardize their bonuses.[25] Thus, in Poland during the 1970s, when the Gierek regime sought to double the country's national product—"build a second Poland!" was the phrase the party-state propagandists coined—it believed it could do so only by borrowing billions of dollars from Western banks and governments, which were to be used to purchase the most up-to-date production technology available. The problem was that the incentive to invest in modern technology from the West was itself corrupt: the "interest in acquiring modern Western technology . . . owed more to the attractions of the foreign travel which its purchase offered than to production considerations."[26] Kazimierz Kloc offers a different, but by no means contradictory, reason for the Polish government's reliance on imported technology: it did not want to have to share power with Polish engineers, as would be likely if it sought to develop more modern technology at home.[27]

Importing innovations from the West depended on permission from the central authorities, permission that could be obtained only by the largest producers possessing the most political influence.[28] These enormous *kombinats*, with their powerful Party cells, are microcosms of the entire regime. Because they cannot be closed, CPEs subsidize the factories that lose the most money. In command economies, it is the economically least efficient firms that the central authorities grant the greatest capacity to innovate.

The process of concentration and centralization of capital, in Marx's vision, is also part of the process of capitalism's class polarization: failed capitalists, i.e. small capitalists, are consigned to the proletariat. This polarization leads to one of Marx's most important predictions about capitalism, the increasing impoverishment of the working class.

Socialist Immiseration and the Rise of the Lumpen-Society

Marx was both fascinated and appalled by what he regarded as the apparent fact that the wealthier the capitalist economy, the worse off workers became. "Accumulation of wealth at one pole is," he says, "at the same time accumulation of misery, the torment of labor, slavery, ignorance, brutalization and moral degradation ... on the side of the class that produces its own product as capital."[29] Marx provides a testable prediction: In capitalism, over time, the standard of living of workers will decline. Powerful rhetoric. But why is it true only under communism?

Interestingly, Marx thinks that competition among capitalist firms, or at least the large ones, increases their income, but competition among workers decreases theirs. The idea that both capitalists and workers could be better off is a contradiction within Marxist thought. That both would be worse off without competition, indeed in the presence of planning, is enough to shatter the entire theoretic enterprise.

No prediction made by Marx, it is possible to argue, is more important, more essential both to his critique and to his analysis of capitalism. No prediction made by Marx, one should add, has been disproved by the real world of capitalism as conclusively as his immiseration thesis. But Marx's immiseration thesis came true in relative as well as absolute terms (relative to the West and relative to their own condition in the 1970s) in countries with communist political economies. Prior to 1989, the quality of life for citizens in Eastern Europe had been declining for at least a decade and a half. Per capita GNP in most, perhaps even all, of these countries declined substantially during the late 1970s and 1980s.[30] Environmental values declined even more.[31]

We find a mechanism for testing predictions here, too. Marx's predictions for the growing impoverishment of society are based on what he calls the "industrial" or "disposable reserve army"[32] formed because "capitalist accumulation ... constantly produces, and produces indeed in the direct relation of its own energy and extent, a relatively redundant working population, i.e., a population which is superfluous to capital's average requirements ... and is therefore a surplus population."[33] It might seem that this is one aspect in which Marx's analyses of capitalism diverge from the reality of communism. Real socialist countries managed to abolish unemployment. Instead, they experience shortages of labor, as they experiences shortages of most other valuable goods. How then can we connect Marx to real socialism?

One answer can be found by looking at the nature of communism's labor shortage. The income of industry depends on meeting and exceeding quotas for production, which are almost always raised from year to year. At the same time, supplies (including labor) allocated by the central planners are inherently uncertain. Thus it pays industry to stock up on labor as well as other inputs. Overmanning is normal. During periodic crackdowns on excess supplies, the existence of an army of underemployed workers is a prime target of reduction. Nevertheless, it benefits factories to stockpile workers, saving them for the periodic bursts of production—"storming"—at the end of the quota period. This gives work a peculiar tempo. During the largest part of a plan period, the pace of production is quite slow. Bottlenecks are the norm, as materials do not arrive when they are supposed to, workers do not come to work all the time, negotiations to alter plan targets continue, and so on. As the end of the plan period nears, however, all stops are pulled out. In order to meet their quotas, managers mobilize all resources available, which means getting all the employees into the plant. Firms in CPEs consequently experience a simultaneous shortage and oversupply of workers. They have too many workers for most of the plan period, but too few at the end. "Shortage induces the firms to hoard labor," Pietsch says in her study of the Soviet Union. "It is an act of prudence for the firm to keep superfluous labor because of the losses caused by turnover and because sooner or later the firm may expand, and the superfluous labor will then be required." Moreover, the frequent bottlenecks mean "a greater reserve army of workers is needed inside the factory ... to compensate for the down-time after the required materials arrive and in order to produce the missing parts themselves."[34] Kornai calls this "unemployment on the job."[35]

In some ways, at the same time that real socialism managed to create universal full-employment, it also managed to make unemployment universal. True, everyone had a job, but most people viewed their jobs as meaningless. Production followed irrational patterns, demands on their time and energy were senseless, their official rewards were almost entirely unrelated to anything that was connected to productivity. Much of the time of workers was spent standing around—if, that is, they were even at work. For most it was more profitable or useful to pursue activities outside of the factory or plant, to work at an unofficial second job or simply to wait in a queue. For most people, one's official job was primarily seen as an opportunity for theft: theft of products that could be sold elsewhere; theft of materials that could be used for personal or private use; theft of time from the state; and theft of social services provided by the state, but for which the worker did not do his part.

In his economic writings, when Marx discusses unemployed people, he talks of an industrial reserve army that drives down wages and increases the intensity of work for the employed. If any worker complained, he could easily be replaced by one of the many jobless. But in Marx's sociological and political writings, he calls the members of the industrial reserve army the "lumpenproletariat." Rather than being an economic concept, the lumpenproletariat is much more of a moral notion. These pathetic individuals, on Marx's account, are the chronically unemployed dregs of capitalist society, the thugs who are hired by capitalists to break up strikes and rough up their employed proletarian comrades:[36]

> It is a recruiting ground for thieves and criminals of all sorts, living off the garbage of society, people without a definite trace, vagabonds, *gens sans feu et sans aveu,* varying according to the cultural level of their particular nation ... capable of the greatest acts of heroism and the most exalted self-sacrifice as well as the lowest forms of banditry and the foulest corruption.[37]

Marx's *lumpenproletariat* is in many ways a terrifying vision of what can happen to individuals when they are deprived of meaningful work. For all his condemnations of capitalist factory life, he clearly believes it is morally better than not working at all.

Disguised unemployment in real socialism meant that Marx's descendants had created nothing less than a "lumpen-society." Deprived of meaningful work, most members of communist society experienced the lack of moral underpinnings that Marx and many others think is provided by production. Work in these countries was believed (correctly) to be senseless.[38] Production was only for the sake of production, not for consumption. It most certainly was not production for the sake of the self-realization of producers, Workers in capitalism, according to Marx's critique, work not for the sake of any inherent pleasure that might be derived from creation, but only for the sake of what they earn in order to buy the bare essentials of life. Yet even this minimal quantum of purpose or meaningfulness was denied workers in real socialism. If most people could have earned more, it would hardly have mattered, since the regime of permanent shortages—the dominant and omnipresent feature of everyday life in CPEs—meant that what counts most could not be acquired at all, or at any rate not legally. Apart from waiting in the ubiquitous queues, for most people goods could only be stolen from work, or acquired by exchanging something stolen from the workplace. After the workplace's utility as a site for special advantage has been exhausted, by and large, work did not pay.

Crime did, however. Alienation manifested itself not only as discontent but as mass criminalization. The alienation experienced in CPEs manifested itself in a profound moral breakdown. Everyone was forced to break the rules everyday simply to make ends meet. Literally everyone was a criminal, for the simple reason that, in a shortage economy, it was impossible to survive without breaking the law. The only way to acquire many essential goods was through illegal channels, from bribery to outright theft. Some critics of capitalism view crime here as resulting from the poor's dissatisfaction with the system, as an expression of their protest against the injustices and inequalities of society. Much of the crime in real socialist countries really was an expression of alienation: alienation from the state, whose laws, whose very existence, were not recognized as legitimate. A state that was perceived as robbing rather than serving or protecting its citizens; alienation from work, since the primary function of the workplace for many people was as a source of goods that could be "privatized." Crime also was an expression of the individual's alienation from the community. Everyone recognized that his crime hurt his fellows and that their crimes hurt him, but at the same time that it would be suicidal to refrain from engaging in the unlawful acquisition of goods and services. It was the deprivation of meaningful work, perhaps more than anything else, that was responsible for the social problems that continue to plague post-communist societies: the high rates of alcoholism, the lack of initiative, the sense of fatalism. It is largely responsible for the moral collapse of communism.

Fetishism and the Inevitability of Systemic Collapse

Perhaps the most celebrated prediction Marx makes of capitalism is that its periodic cycles of economic crisis will lead to the system's collapse. Obviously, capitalism has not collapsed yet, and, equally obviously, communism has. It is possible to go beyond saying that the predictions Marx made for the development of capitalism have come to pass in real socialism. The reasons communism could not stave off its terminal crises, why it was never able to get off "the treadmill of reforms,"[39] can be illuminated by Marx's account of capitalism's fate. One place to begin is with Marx's notion of fetishism. Capitalism's institutions, Marx says, obscure the true nature of social relations. Most famous of these institutions is the commodity. According to Marx, because of the nature of capitalist production, in which things are more important than people, the commodities made by humans appear to possess the qualities of living beings. We might note in passing that in communist countries, this happens to be true. CPEs do not ration investment by varying the cost of capital (i.e., interest rates), relying instead on a struggle among powerful producers for inputs to fulfill their quotas. The result is chronic shortage for those with the least clout—consumers. Observers are struck by how often hunting metaphors are used by those who must try to find life's necessities in a shortage economy. No one in these countries talks about trying to find toilet paper or furniture the way they might try to find pretty pebbles on a beach. You don't look for towels or curtains as you would in a Western store. You *stalk* them. The imagery evoked in acquiring goods is of a prey that is clever, resourceful, and elusive.[40]

At the same time that commodities in capitalism are invested with living properties, Marx believes, their creators become less human. They see themselves more and more as passive things. This too happens to be true in communist economies. Although some people pride themselves on being shrewd and canny in their acquisition of scarce goods, more often consumers see the hunt as an activity determined by fortune and misfortune, one in which the results are entirely out of the control of ordinary people. What is interesting about Marx's notion of the fetishism of commodities applied to real socialism is not so much that individuals misinterpret economic reality—no one really thinks commodities are alive—but rather that a sense of fatalism is reinforced among the inhabitants of communist countries, a fatalism that expresses itself as overwhelming resignation.[41] While they view themselves as passive recipients of whatever fate will allow them a chance to buy on any given day, however, few of the hunters are unaware of the cause of the permanent shortages with which they must live every day: it is nothing less than the system of real socialism itself.

Marx himself realizes that people, do not usually treat commodities like fetishes or religious artifacts.[42] A more interesting and important use of fetishism is that of capital, of investment, and accumulation. According to Marx, "In interest-bearing capital, the capital relationship reaches its most ... fetishized form."[43] In capital fetishism, capital appears to be autonomously productive in and of itself, regardless of the activity of humans, which Marx believes is the true source of value. Of course, everyone would agree that unless at least some capital is invested productively, there will be no interest. From the perspective of the financial capitalist, however, this doesn't matter, since, as Marx conceived him, he is totally separated from the process whereby value is produced. He will continue to invest so as to accrue interest because that is what is economically rational to do. Regardless of what he believes (Marx knows that he would have to look for a long time to find anyone who actually believes production of valuable goods and services is unrelated to the productivity of capital), the finance capitalist will act as though he believes his capital will expand without being invested productively.

Thus we see that, in this account of fetishism, it makes no difference what particular beliefs individuals hold. Presumably, a capitalist who believes her investment is productive because of magic inherent in capital will invest no differently than the capitalist who does not believe this. At least, this indifference to experience is implied by Marx's view that capitalism impels people by impersonal laws. What matters is the structure of social and economic institutions. So it is with commodity fetishism. It does not make a difference if people really ascribe to commodities the fetishistic properties Marx describes. What matters is that they act as though they think commodities are more important than people, and that they pursue the increase in resources that commodities represent with the same single-minded devotion that a religious adherent might pursue a holy relic.

Even taking into account the proviso that investment fetishism does not require capitalists actually to believe what Marx says they believe, it still does not accurately explain what happens in capitalism. Imagine the capitalist who invests without getting production to show for his investment. At a certain point creditors must be repaid; if he cannot he will go, as is so pungently said, belly up.

However absurd Marx's claim about investment fetishism in capitalism, it is correct in characterizing real socialism. In communist economies, the road to material reward—for workers, managers, planners, and Party chiefs—is paved not with production but with investment. Paradoxically, greater and greater investment means less and less growth. To say the same thing slightly differently, greater investment in real socialism is constantly accompanied by the perception of unending capital shortages. Investment in these countries shows a tendency to increase, even when it clearly leads to lower productivity. For workers and managers, reward comes from production—meeting the quota, not satisfying consumers or producing goods that work. For planners, fortune comes from projecting new investment, so there will be economic growth, at least on paper.

At an extreme, a firm that makes poor decisions without correcting for them will go out of business. As Marx knew, capitalism is inherently Darwinian. According to Armen Alchian, economists cannot rely on the notion of "profit-maximization," since this implies a sort of certainty that neither economic actors nor economists can possess. Instead, we can speak only of "positive realized profits" which allow a firm to stay in business. In a competitive environment, Alchian says, bankruptcy serves as a selection mechanism paralleling Darwin's mechanism of selective survival in biology. Even if capitalists made investment decisions at random, in a competitive economy we could be sure that profitable (thus productive) investments would be the ones made by firms that happened to stay afloat.[44]

Look at these selection mechanisms from the point of view of a Marxist contrasting Marx's vision of communism with contemporary capitalism. Many, if not most of the choices of investment projects in capitalism seem to Marxists wasteful, inefficient, in some cases even immoral. So too are the devices that select or weed out projects. The most obvious candidates for elimination in the ideal social order are profits and bankruptcy, upon which most of these mechanisms of choice rest. Profit, according to the Marxist, is the source of much of capitalism's injustice.

And yet, far from fettering the development of the forces of production, these market mechanisms have been able to prevent the collapse of the system. In the language of systems theory, the instability of the parts (profitseeking firms) helps secure the stability of the whole (the capitalist market). Conversely, socialism's unwillingness to allow its parts (the megaministries, the *kombinats*, the enormous and enormously inefficient enterprises and factories) to decline or disappear, has resulted in negative selective, dooming the command economy to collapse. The task for Marx's followers would be to devise ways for the post-capitalist economy to ensure the productivity of investment without relying on the search for profit or on bankruptcy. Without doing this, falling prey to the fetish of investments described by Marx would be inevitable. And so, in CPEs, it has proved to be.

Why Trust Is a Problem in Communism

Marx's misunderstanding of how institutions could arise without being planned by society as a whole can be seen in his view of trust. It is capitalism's lack of trust that contributes to the capitalist's oppression of his employees. How else to get them to work, when all their interests are conflicting? Capitalists themselves cannot trust one another. The hatred of their instrumental social relations is seen in Marx's passionate, eloquent, but wrong-headed denunciation of credit in capitalism. "Credit," says Marx, "is a self-estrangement, a dehumanization, all the more infamous and extreme because its element is no longer a commodity, metal or paper, but the moral existence, the social existence, the very heart of man, and because under the appearance of mutual trust between men it is really the greatest distrust and a total estrangement."[45] Freeing society of market relations, Marx and his followers claim, would free people of alienation. In a true community of equals, it seems, in a community in which people can trust their fellows, there will be no need for institutions like credit, any more than there be the need for bosses forcing workers to work. Marx's view of money as eroding trust is similar.

When Lenin and his comrades took power in Russia, they had not thought through what would be required to create a working socialist economy. On one level, they believed they could create communism by abolishing money relations in favor of direct exchange of goods. The result was the economic disaster called "war communism."[46] Their inability to construct an economy based on use-values rather than exchange-values revealed and foreshadowed a basic feature of real socialism that was to continue well after the abandonment of war communism, until real socialism's recent collapse: an inability to construct institutions of trust. For someone like Marx, it is likely that the phrase, "institutions of trust," would be an oxymoron. He certainly does not approve of the erosion of trust represented in his view by the capitalist institutions of money and credit. But in any modern economy exchanges must take place across group boundaries and across geographic distances. Face-to-face dealings with a known acquaintance are not always possible. Marx might think that with the coming of socialism will also come a "new socialist man" who is entirely trustworthy. This item of faith never helped those of his followers who had to construct ways of trusting each other in the here-and-now.

In the late eighteenth and early nineteenth centuries, to consider the United States for a moment, Lynne Zucker argues, a combination of many social changes—including the geographic expansion of the economy, mass immigration, the rise of new industries—served to erode previous ways of ensuring trust in one's transaction partners. Relying on reputation and a common family and ethnic background no longer sufficed. As a result, "a market for trust" developed:

> new organizations, designed to rebuild, to produce trust. Through institutionalizing socially created mechanisms for producing trust, the economic order was gradually reconstructed. First, rational bureaucratic procedures were adopted to provide written rules and a formal hierarchy that provided trust between employers and employees. Second, professional certification became widespread, with credentialing replacing informal "reputation." Third, a distinctive economic sector, the social overhead capital sector or producers services, arose to bridge transactions between firms and between individuals and firms. This sector includes banking, insurance, government, real estate, and legal services. Fourth, regulation and legislation established a common framework, including general expectations and specific rules governing transactions.[47]

However many problems these institutions have encountered, it is difficult to imagine the economy functioning without them. Moreover, looking outside the United States reveals even more innovative institutions for the production of trust: Think of the Japanese system of "lifetime-employment" (for at least some workers), the Taiwanese structure of interlinking family firms, Swedish social democratic corporatism. Capitalism has given the opportunities and rewards for different social orders to experiment with new institutions.

The ability of individuals to develop novel organizational forms is excluded in a communist political economy, where the right to create new organizations is jealously guarded by the center. In CPEs, one institution is primarily responsible for the production of trust: the *nomenklatura,* the vetting of individuals who might be given any responsible position in society by organs of the party-state. As originally conceived, the *nomenklatura* was intended to test moral character.[48] The *nomenklatura* in advanced socialism degenerated into a privileged clique concerned only with protecting its members. As the communist system lost its commitment to Marxism, admission to the *nomenklatura* came to represent not ideological purity, but rather nothing more than a demonstrated willingness to compromise oneself for the sake of personal advancement. The point was not to identify independent thinking in order to foster it, but rather to identify it in order to ensure such thinking would not contaminate the ruling circles. Sitting through the obligatory courses in Marxist-Leninist doctrine—when everyone knew it was for no reason other than seeking to get into the corridors of privilege and power—and parroting the doctrinal line propounded in them taught the prospective member next to nothing about Marx. But it showed the authorities that the candidate was willing to do anything for the sake of rising in the hierarchy—he was a good sort of person to admit into your club if you wanted to avoid upsetting things. In Poland and other CPEs, it served as a way of cementing individuals into rival patron-client networks. What resulted, then, was the moral *and* material failure so evident in the 1980s.[49] Concentrating "trust" in one particular body while denying society the opportunities to develop new organizations led to the corruption of trust in the one place where it was intended: in the party-state where only fellow thieves trusted one another.

Again we see that a monopoly of the right to create new formal structures by the rulers led to the inability to change their system, even though for many years they all knew it was crumbling. The mechanisms of the *nomenklatura* insured that the "untrustworthy"—which is to say, potentially innovative individuals who might endanger the system or the various patronage networks within the system—would be excluded from the levers of power. Concentration of power within the party-state meant that society was unable to develop formal mechanisms for the production of trust that could substitute for face-to-face dealings by friends, family and acquaintances.

Why It Matters that Marx's Predictions Intended of Capitalism Have Come True for Communism

Under the rules for the transition from the old to the new order, the operational embodiment of communism, the command economy, became a vulgar imitation of capitalism.[50] The Communist Party sought to create the material productivity that Marx believed to be a prerequisite to communism and Stalin thought would enable the Soviet Union to catch up with the more developed and hostile capitalist West. The Soviets could do so, they thought, only by copying the capitalists' ways of accumulation. Partly because they believed capitalists extracted their unearned surplus from the proletariat through force and fraud, they set out to do so more directly (Marx and his followers prided themselves on the transparency of their social relations) and more forcefully.

In constructing their version of vulgar capitalism, however, the communist creators left out what they hated most about capitalism: interest rates to ration capital, private property and capital markets to buy and sell businesses, and market prices to direct production to consumer desires. All these mechanisms were, in the eyes of Marx's children, anarchic, irrational, messy. Their functions could be filled much better by all-knowing and all-powerful central allocators. Unfortunately, what they most hated turned out to be most valuable, or, at least, essential. Marx writes that capitalist economies would collapse because the material forces of production come into conflict with the social relations of production. In essence, he claims, technological development and economic growth forces a change in property rights. Broadly speaking, his theory is right on the mark. What is important to realize is that it is administered decisions, which reach their most sublime development in the command economy, that are at odds with economic growth.

Rather than going over the well-known economic reasons for communism's collapse—perverse incentives, the inability to innovate, and the like—our intention of assessing the ability of Marx's theory to predict and explain the fall of communism will be better served by looking at the major Marxist blind spot, namely, organizational politics. Actually, Marxian-cum-Leninist politics has been extremely interested in the Communist Party as (to use Selznick's apt phrase) "organizational weapon," a "combat party" that can be directed against adversaries abroad, at home, and within the Party.[51] What is missing? *There is no discussion of how to deal with supporters.* The reason is, it seems, self-evident: Supporters are supposed to be supportive. The interests of the proletariat, as interpreted by its vanguard, the Communist Party, are supposed to be universal. Doubting this fundamental truth would mean doubting the Party's right to rule. On this line of thinking, constructing mechanisms to cement the support of supporters would be a potentially self-destructive expression of doubt. Among the many ironies of communism's imitation of Marx's capitalism is that the internal Party hierarchy violated the most distinctive feature of Marxism-Leninism-Stalinism: perpetual class warfare. The one place where class warfare was disallowed, namely, inside the *nomenklatura,* proved the party-state's undoing.

The problem of factions in Leninist Parties could never be resolved. Unlike the Madisonian approach to factions enshrined in the American Constitution, which recognizes that factions go together with freedom and that the best solution is to try to control the most dangerous and damaging aspects of factional conflict, "Lenin sought to remove the cause rather [than] control the effects of faction."[52] The very existence of factions within the Party could never be recognized. Hence, it never occurred to Party theorists to ask what they would do when all organizations, from factories to government agencies, were dominated by their own supporters: Party members, including factory managers, bureaucrats, secret police, elite workers. How could one go against these constituents? Closing a factory or agency would be like killing one's own child, for these organizations are microcosms of communist regimes. No possibility of "tough love" here; as factories and agencies grow ever larger and less efficient, the regime correspondingly declines. Were these offenses committed by enemies,[53] the party-state would know exactly what to do: Stalin and his descendants were, after all, very efficient in dealing with sabotage committed by real or imagined "class enemies." But when the regime itself is responsible for its own sabotage? When the weakening of the regime results from its own organization (another example of the parts undermining the whole), the community party-state is helpless. Capitalism, when it works—when, that is, the parts do not manage to shelter themselves from competition—does kill the things it loves: unprofitable businesses do go under, which means the market grows stronger. The inability of communist parties (not normally thought of as sentimental creatures) to kill their own has resulted in their own deaths.

Now we can see why Marx's predictions have come true under communism. The basic explanation is that assumptions about capitalism made by Marx and his followers are much more true about real socialism. Think about it: a ruling group caring for more about its privileges and power than about those over whom it rules; the complete interpenetration of economic and politics, with the one controlling the other; the division of society into the few who rule and the many who they oppress; the mobilization of opinion manipulation by church, school, media, etc., in the service of the regime; the punishment and marginalization of dissidents; the unshakable position of forces leading inexorably to giganticism. We see elements of all these to some degree in some capitalist countries at some times. But they are the very foundation of the communist political economy, from its formation to its eventual collapse.

Marxist theory, we know, was developed by highly intelligent people. It has been subjected to critical review from within and without for many decades. The result, to its credit, has been considerable internal theoretic coherence: for the most part, the conclusions (in the form of explanations and predictions) do flow from the premises. The problem is that Marxian premises are far more true for communism than for capitalism. And that remarkable congruence came about because the rulers of what was, until very recently, the Union of Soviet Socialist Republics built their system—the dictatorship of the command economy—upon their distorted vision of what capitalism was like.

The rejection of political pluralism (beginning with Marx and running through Lenin, Stalin, and Brezhnev) virtually guaranteed that the Soviet regime and its imitators would make good on another of Marx's diagnoses and predictions, namely, the mystification of the masses. According to Marx, the bourgeoisie pretended to be no more than citizens in a liberal democracy possessing no more rights and powers than any other citizens, while in fact they ruled in a capitalist dictatorship. An enormous amount of the resources of the capitalist state, mass media, and social institutions like schools and churches are devoted to fostering this illusion, which Antonio Gramsci and his followers call "bourgeois ideological hegemony." The same mystification exists in CPEs, only in a much more pronounced manner. The populace is told that the Communist Party acts in its interests, *is* its interests, corresponding to the universal class that transcends all narrow interests. In reality, as became apparent to all, the Party acted only in its own interest. This was shown by the fact that the higher up in the Party one rose, the easier it was to *escape* communism—escape the dinginess through easy travel to the West, escape the ubiquitous queues through special shops, escape contact with one's subjects through special Party vacation resorts, escape the mystifications through greater access to genuine information.

As long as the Party remained the sole legally sanctioned source of power, force was required to prevent opposition. Thus, those gifted in coercion rose to the top. Because the vulgar capitalism that passes for socialism is ill-suited for economic growth, coercion has to be applied in increasing doses. It is ever more difficult to buy the support, or even passivity, of the masses when the economy is crumbling. Instead of the considerable inequality of wealth and power existing in most democracies, the vulgar capitalism called communism carried these tendencies to an extreme—perhaps the greatest extreme ever seen in modern times. Marx's predictions for capitalism were realized in communist political economies because his assumptions about capitalism fit the communist model much better. For one thing, the factors offsetting and, to some extent mitigating, the inequalities produced and reproduced by capitalism—higher and, over time, improving standards of living, considerable upward and downward mobility, a rule of law guaranteeing most citizens relatively equal access to legal redress, a political system allowing even the underprivileged some say in matters affecting them, and the excitement of political and economic innovation—were absent under vulgar capitalism. For another, the lack of continuous economic progress, which increased discontent, thereby elicited more repression from the state, which even further increased society's tendency to reject the system. All this gives the regime an excuse to delay its declaration that full communism has been achieved, a declaration that would be important because it would officially signal the end of repression. During what became a prolonged transition period to Marx's version of genuine communism, it turned out that the treatment meted out to class enemies, the complete asymmetry of political power, and the increasing impoverishment of large parts of the population amidst increasing privilege for the *nomenklatura,* proved to be remarkably similar to what Marx prophesied for capitalism.

Marx thought that, in capitalism, all the unequal rewards and power being increasing concentrated within a small group of people would lead to working class consciousness. It would reveal to the masses that the ideological mystifications were falsehoods, that all they would have to do in order to rid society of its inequalities and inefficiencies is to attack this ruling class and democratize the source of its power. For Marx, this demystification would be a recognition of workers that they would have to democratize capital; then all the other inequalities and injustices would fall as well. The fact that so many privileges and powers were monopolized by the political elite in communist political economies meant that this prediction too came to pass. Every day, in every area of life—from the time they got up to an apartment without heat to the hours they had to stand in line for food, from the humiliating experience of seeing those with no qualifications besides political connection making boneheaded decisions in the factory, to the equally humiliating experience of having to play up to these political hacks for the merest of favors—society in CPEs was reminded of who had power, and why. Thus, a Western Marxist intellectual who actually worked for several years in Hungarian factories, notes: "Ironically, then, workers are more likely to recover a socialist consciousness and struggle to appropriate control over production and distribution of surplus under state socialism than under capitalism. That is, such control struggles are endemic to state socialism."[54] And so it happened across the communist world.

Notes

[1] The close fit between the condemnations levelled by Marx and Marxists against capitalism and the reality of communist political economies (CPEs) like Poland was the subject of John Clark and Aaron Wildavsky, *The Moral Collapse of Communism: Poland as a Cautionary Tale* (San Francisco: Institute for Contemporary Studies, 1990).

[2] For instance, Vladimir Bukovsky, "Totalitarianism in Crisis: Is There a Smooth Transition to Democracy?" in Ellen Frankel Paul, ed. *Totalitarianism at the Crossroads* (New Brunswick: Transaction Books, 1991): 9–30.

[3] Adam Michnik, "Nowy ewolucjonizm," in Michnik, *Szanse Polskiej Demokracji: Artykuly i Eseje* (London: Aneks, 1984): 80. While awaiting trial in 1985, Michnik anticipated the events that were in a few years to catch everyone else unawares. Of those who assume communism "can continue forever," Michnik said: "They forget the inevitability of surprise in the very nature of the Leading System. Here, on a spring morning, one may wake up in a totally changed country. Here—more than once—Party buildings have burned while commissars escaped clad only in underwear." "Letter from the Gdansk Prison, 1985," in Adam Michnik, *Letters from Prison and Other Essays* (Berkeley: University of California Press, 1985): 98.

[4] A point graphically illustrated by the tables on quality of life presented by Brzezinski, who contrasts countries that were at similar levels of economic development in 1960—the Soviet Union and Japan; West Germany, East Germany, and Czechoslovakia; Spain and Poland; Italy and Yugoslavia; Austria and Hungary; India and China—showing just how much deterioration the communist countries experienced relative to their noncommunist counterparts. Zbigniew Brzezinski, *The Grand Failure: The Birth and Death of Communism in the Twentieth Century* (New York: Charles Scribner's Sons, 1989): 259–270.

[5]N. Scott Arnold, *Marx's Radical Critique of Capitalist Society: A Reconstruction and Critical Evaluation* (Oxford: Oxford University Press, 1990).

[6]A sense of the bewildering variety of these versions, as well as the often inbred and incestuous debates among the different theorists, can be found in Paul Bellis, *Marxism in the U.S.S.R.: The Theory of Proletarian Democracy and the Marxist Analysis of Soviet Society* (Atlantic Highlands, NJ: Humanities Press, 1979). Less painfully detailed treatments include Adam Buick and William Jerome, "Soviet State Capitalism? The History of an Idea," *Survey* 62 (January 1967): Adam Westoby, "Conceptions of Communist States," in David Held, et al., ed. *States and Societies* (New York: New York University Press, 1983): 219–240.

[7]Ferenc Feher, Agnes Heller, and Gyorgy Markus, *Dictatorship over Needs: An Analysis of Soviet Societies* (Oxford: Blackwell, 1983): 23.

[8]Karl Marx, *Value, Price and Profit* (New York: International Publishers, 1935): 39.

[9]Fred M. Gottheil, *Marx's Economic Predictions* (Evanston: Northwestern University Press, 1966).

[10]See Pauline Marie Vaillancourt, *When Marxists Do Research* (New York: Greenwood Press, 1986); and Pauline M. Rosenau, "Philosophy, Methodology, and Research: Marxist Assumptions about Inquiry," *Comparative Political Studies* 20:4 (January 1988): 423–454.

[11]Georg Lukacs, *History and Class Consciousness: Studies in Marxist Dialectics* (Cambridge, Mass.: The MIT Press, 1971): 1.

[12]Max Weber, "Science as a Vocation," in Hans H. Gerth and C. Wright Mills, ed. *From Max Weber: Essays in Sociology* (New York: Oxford University Press, 1946): 138.

[13]These important debates are summarized in W. H. Newton-Smith, *The Rationality of Science* (London: Routledge and Kegan Paul, 1981).

[14]Karl R. Popper, *The Logic of Scientific Discovery* (London: Hutchinson, 1968; Imre Lakatos, "Falsification and the Methodology of Scientific Research Programmes," in Alan Musgrave and Imre Lakatos, ed. *Criticism and the Growth of Knowledge* (Cambridge: Cambridge University Press, 1970): 91–196.

[15]Thomas S. Kuhn, *The Structure of Scientific Revolutions,* 2nd ed. (Chicago: University of Chicago Press, 1970).

[16]Karl Marx, *Grundrisse,* Martin Nicholaus, trans. (New York: Vintage Books, 1973): 748.

[17]*Grundrisse,* 754.

[18]Simon Clarke, "The Marxist Theory of Overaccumulation and Crisis," *Science and Society* 54:4 (Winter 1990–91): 445–446.

[19]Karl Marx, *Capital,* v. III. David Fernbach, trans. (New York: Vintage Books, 1981): 318–319.

[20]Clarke, 447.

[21]Karl Marx, *Capital*, v. I, Ben Fowkes, trans. (New York: Vintage Books): 739–779.

[22]*Ibid.*, 777.

[23]Jane Marceau, "The Dwarves of Capitalism: The Structure of Production and the Economic Culture of the Small Manufacturing Firm," in Stewart R. Clegg and S. Gordon Redding, ed. *Capitalism in Contrasting Cultures* (New York: Walter de Gruyter, 1990): 373. For more detail, see R. Oakley, *High Technology Small Firms* (London: Frances Pinter, 1986).

[24]Marco Orru, "The Institutional Logic of Small-firm Economies in Italy and Taiwan," *Studies in Comparative International Development* 26:1 (Spring 1991): 3–28.

[25]See Joseph S. Berliner, *The Innovation Decision in Soviet Industry* (Cambridge, Mass.: The MIT Press, 1976); and Bruce Parrott, *Politics and Technology in the Soviet Union* (Cambridge, Mass.: The MIT Press, 1983).

[26]Tomasz Stankiewicz, "Investment under Socialism," *Communist Economies* 1:2 (1989): 124.

[27]Kazimierz Kloc, "Nie straszmy sie samorzadem" [Let's not be afraid of self-government], *Przeglad Techniczny* 33–34 (1981): 10–13.

[28]See Jan Winiecki, "Soviet-Type Economies' Strategy for Catching-up Through Technology Imports: An Anatomy of Failure," *Technovation* 6:2 (June 1987).

[29]*Capital*, I, 799.

[30]See Thad P. Alton, "East European GNPs, Domestic Final Uses of Gross Product, Rates of Growth, and International Comparisons," in *Pressures for Reform in the East European Economies* (Washington: Joint Economic Committee of the United States Congress, 1989): 77–96.

[31]See Sabine Rosenbladt, "Is Poland Lost?" *Greenpeace* 13:6 (December, 1988): 14–19; and Sabine Rosenbladt, "Environmental Concerns in Poland," in Gale Stokes, ed. *From Stalinism to Pluralism: A Documentary History of Eastern Europe since 1945* (Oxford: Oxford University Press, 1991): 188–192.

[32]*Capital*, I, 784.

[33]*Ibid.*, 782.

[34]Anna-Jutta Pietsch, "Shortage of Labour and Motivation Problems of Soviet Workers," in David Lane, ed. *Labour and Employment in the U.S.S.R.* (Washington Square, NY: New York University Press, 1986): 186–187.

[35]Janos Kornai, *The Economics of Shortage* (Amsterdam: North-Holland, 1980): 254.

[36]For examples of this role for the lumpenproletariat, see "Agitation against the Sunday Trading Bill," in Karl Marx, *Surveys from Exile,* David Fernbach, ed. (New York: Vintage Books, 1974): 296.

[37]"The Class Struggles in France: 1848 to 1850," in *Surveys from Exile,* 52–53.

[38]According to the Polish government's surveys of the Lenin shipyard in Gdansk before the outbreak of Solidarity in 1980, 40 to 60 hours of each worker's monthly work time was spent looking for or waiting for tools and materials (time for which they were not paid). Roman Laba, *The Roots of Solidarity: A Political Sociology of Poland's Working Class Democratization* (Princeton: Princeton University Press, 1991): 122.

[39]The phrase comes from Gertrude Schroeder, "The Soviet Economy on a Treadmill of 'Reforms,'" in *The Soviet Economy in Time of Change* (Washington: Joint Economic Committee of the United States Congress, 1979).

[40]See chapters 5, 6, and 7 of *The Moral Collapse of Communism.*

[41]Fatalists believe that human nature is unpredictable and physical nature operates at random, thereby justifying their passivity. The haphazard operation of the command economy would be enough to make anyone a fatalist. See Michael Thompson, Richard Ellis, and Aaron Wildavsky, *Cultural Theory* (Boulder: Westview Press, 1990), chapter 12: "The Missing Ways of Life: Egalitarianism and Fatalism," 223–232; and Edward C. Banfield, *The Moral Basis of a Backward Society* (New York: The Free Press, 1958).

[42]"This mystification," he says, "is still a very simple one in the case of a commodity. Everybody understands more or less clearly that the relations of commodities as exchange-values are really the relations of people to the productive activities of one another." Karl Marx, *A Contribution to the Critique of Political Economy* (Moscow: Progress Publishers, 1958): 22.

[43]*Capital,* III, 515.

[44]Armen A. Alchian, *Economic Forces at Work* (Indianapolis: Liberty Press, 1977): 15–36.

[45]"Excerpts from James Mill's *Elements of Political Economy*," in Karl Marx, *Early Writings* (New York: Vintage Books, 1975): 263–265.

[46]For a very good recent analysis, see Peter Boettke, *The Political Economy of Soviet Socialism: The Formative Years, 1918–1928* (Boston: Kluwer Academic Publishers, 1990).

[47]Lynne G. Zucker, "Production of Trust: Institutional Sources of Economic Structure, 1840–1920," *Research in Organizational Behavior,* v. I (1986): 55.

[48]See Michael Voslensky, *Nomenklatura: Anatomy of the Soviet Ruling Class* (London: The Bodley Head, 1984).

[49]The degeneration of the *nomenklatura* is discussed by Jacek Tarlowski in "Patronage in a Centralized, Socialist System: The Case of Poland," *International Political Science Review* 4:4 (1983): 495–518; "Old and New Patterns of Corruption in Poland and the U.S.S.R.," *Telos* 80 (Summer 1989): 51–62.

[50]We have argued this point in greater detail in John Clark and Aaron Wildavsky, "Why Communism Collapses: The Moral and Material Failures of Command Economies are Intertwined," *Journal of Public Policy* 10:4 (October-December 1990): 361–390.

[51]Philip Selznick, *The Organizational Weapon: A Study of Bolshevik Strategy and Tactics* (New York: McGraw-Hill, 1952).

[52]Carl Linden, "Opposition and Faction in Communist Party Leaderships," in Frank Belloni and Dennis C. Beller, eds. *Faction Politics: Political Parties and Factionalism in Comparative Perspective* (Santa Barbara, CA: ABC-CLIO, 1978): 363.

[53]As in the joke: In the waning days of the Cold War, a CIA agent shares a drink with his former counterpart in the KGB. "Tell the truth," the Soviet spy says, "You were responsible for Chernobyl, right?" "No," replies the CIA man, "but Gosplan—that was our idea."

[54]Michael Burawoy, *The Politics of Production: Factory Regimes under Capitalism and Socialism* (London: Verso, 1985): 197.

Vladimir Bukovsky

Yeltsin's First Hundred Days

As the crisis in Moscow once again hit the news in 1992
and early 1993 there was a panic in the Western capitals as
well as among the Russian "democrats." Some hastened to
pronounce what was always expected and feared, yet hoped
to be averted by a miracle—the death of post-August democracy in Russia. Others argued that it was still-born right
from the start, or even that it was never quite a democracy.
But the general feeling was that, whatever it had been, it
was effectively dead now, and whatever was replacing it was
certainly going to be far worse. Many even likened the
change to what had happened seventy-five years earlier,
when a provisional government had been overthrown by the
Bolsheviks; only this time they did it without a single shot
and, hopefully, this time they are not going to stay for the
next 75 years.

Needless to say, historic parallels are more often mislead-
ing than enlightening. While Yeltsin's leadership in his first
one hundred days can be compared with the provisional
government of 1917, both being weak and indecisive, the
present-day "Bolsheviks" are but a pale copy of the Lenin's
"professional revolutionaries." If nothing else, they are even
more split, more confused, and less popular than the
"democrats." They are defeated forces of the past, not the
harbingers of the future, and their agenda does not go further than the dreams of restoration.

So, what then, happened in Moscow in 1992 and early 1993? Nothing much, in my view, except that the crisis deepened even further, and it became apparent even to Yeltsin's "democrats" that they had wasted the few opportunities the August of 1991 "godsend" offered.

The formidable problems of transition from the decades of communist totalitarianism to democracy and market economy are too obvious to discuss here in great detail. On the one hand, there are the challenges presented by "collectivized" agriculture, the "giants of the socialist industry" (both monopolistic and unproductive by their very design), the huge military-industrial complex, the lack of investment capital, depleted resources and, correspondingly, masses of low-skilled laborers who had never worked productively in their lives. (In 1987 workers in industry and agriculture accounted for 61.8 percent of the total population of the U.S.S.R. Collective farmers and intelligentsia accounted for 12 percent and 26.2 percent respectively.)[1] Clearly, any attempt at restructuring such an economy, no matter how gradual and cautious it may be, is bound to create enormous turmoil, reduce the living standards of a sizable majority and generate a huge wave of social discontent. No elected government on earth is likely to survive such a reform, as no elected government could have created such an economy in the first place.

On the other hand, a society emerging from a totalitarian nightmare usually has no political or social structures capable of stabilizing it in transition except those created by and tainted by the totalitarian system. And they are most likely to oppose the changes, thus contributing to political instability typical for all post-totalitarian countries. The new institutions, although numerous and noisy, are usually tiny and weak to the point of merely symbolic existence. They are no match for the well-entrenched, all-pervasive, mafia-like structures evolving from the old regime. They are even too small to replace the governing apparatus and, therefore, the old *nomenklatura* remains in control of all executive functions of a presumably new "democratic" state.

It should be remembered that what we call *"nomenklatura"* is not just an ordinary bureaucracy, but a whole stratum of the society, (18 million strong according to some estimates), with its own vested interests, its own connections with the West, its own accumulated wealth and its own complicity in past crimes to unite its members. Its mere existence poses a real threat to fragile democracy, to say nothing of its control over the executive branch of the government. Add endless ethnic conflicts, fantastic corruption, skyrocketing crime rate, general apathy of the demoralized population, and the task of transition becomes all but impossible.

Also, let us not forget the less than friendly attitude of the West to attempts at establishing democracy in the former Soviet Union. While those who, like Gorbachev and his lot, strived to rescue the moribund communist system and equally doomed Union were given every assistance (including financial support to the tune of $45 billion!), their opponents were vilified right from the start as "unpredictable," "unbalanced," and "dangerous."

Ridiculous as it may seem today, the West has done everything in its power to prolong the agony of the totalitarian system, thus driving the country deeper and deeper into a crisis and making the task of transition more and more difficult. And when this insanity finally stopped, it was not because the West wised up, but because the object of its generosity ceased to exist.

Still, I am convinced that, all these odds notwithstanding, the post-August 1991 democracy, or whatever one may call it, has had a change of survival (and even of a reasonable success) if not for the colossal blunders made by Yeltsin and his team.

April of 1991

Tragically, they made their main conceptual mistake well before August by choosing a way of compromise and evolution rather than that of confrontation and revolution. It was a mistake so fundamental, so much determined by their "class-oriented narrow-mindedness" that we probably should not call it that name. Rather, to borrow Lenin's terminology, we should call it a conscious choice of the people who "still could not rise above their class consciousness." Being themselves a part of *nomenklatura*, they were more afraid of the people than of the Party when popular revolution knocked at the door.

By the end of 1990 it became abundantly clear that the Soviet regime was heading for catastrophe: While Gorbachev's "*perestroika*" failed to deliver what was expected of it by its architects, it did unleash the forces leading to erosion of the regime's foundations. The Soviet empire was in turmoil. From the Baltic Sea to the Caucasian Mountains and from the Danube to Siberia, former "captive nations" were rising up, demanding national independence. In Russia itself, elections to the Soviets of all levels, restricted and manipulated as they were, showed a clear vote of no confidence in the Communist Party. Hundreds of thousands of its members were quitting the ranks, while thousands were publicly burning their membership cards.

Furthermore, a wave of strikes was gathering momentum, threatening to grow into a general strike and to lead to the formation of Solidarity-type labor unions. Clearly, what was not far enough for economic revival was proving to be too far for the regime's political survival; what was intended as a limited within-the-system readjustment was threatening to grow into a popular revolution.

But it was also becoming clear that the regime was preparing to defend itself by all means, including brutal force. In fact, the first signs of this preparation were in evidence as early as 1988 and became obvious by the end of 1989. Most radical elements of the reforms, such as the deregulation of prices and further decentralization, were already suspended. New restrictive laws were hastily introduced, curbing freedom of public meetings, limiting freedom of the press, restricting cooperatives and, above all, extending to the Soviet Army the power of the police. Then, new emergency laws banning strikes, more restrictions on cooperatives, and a decision to increase the number of the Interior Troops followed. Everything seemed to be ready for a crackdown.

In spite of all that, and even after the massacres in Tbilisi (1989) and Baku (1990) had shown that Gorbachev was quite prepared to spill the blood, Yeltsin still hoped to work out a compromise. Only when his last attempt to push through a modest reform program ("500 Days") in the fall of 1990 had been blocked by Gorbachev, and when most of the reform-minded leaders had been replaced by obvious thugs in the sweeping reshuffle of December 1990, was he forced to abandon this hope. Within a month, Gorbachev went onto the offensive: He curtailed *glasnost,* ordered a crackdown on private business activity, robbed old-age pensioners of their life savings, and organized a massacre in the Baltic states. Thus, confrontation between the people on the one hand, and the Party on the other became inevitable.

By a twist of the fate, this meant what Yeltsin tried to avoid: a personal confrontation between him and Gorbachev, the former being a symbol of the people and the latter of the Party. While Yeltsin had the courage to subject himself to the judgment of the nation and received a popular mandate, Gorbachev never took the risk, and he became a hostage of the Party. That fact, more than anything else, determined their subsequent political evolution. Reflecting the difference in their respective power bases, Gorbachev had to hold together a disintegrating empire and to resist any further reforms, even if it required violence and repres-

sion, while Yeltsin had to support the republics in their rebellion against the center and to advocate radical economic
reforms. One chose democracy and left the Party; the other
had no choice but to defend the Party to the bitter end.

By the end of 1990 and the beginning of 1991, Yeltsin
was the only credible leader of the democratic opposition
in Russia. Whether he liked it or not, he had to lead the
country into a confrontation with the old regime. The truth
is, however, contrary to a popular perception both at home
and abroad, he disliked that role and was ill-suited for it.
Being a Party bureaucrat through and through, he could
not imagine politics outside the Party, and he lacked a vision
of a nonsocialist democratic future. Above all, his natural
tendency was to solve problems by compromise, not by confrontation. Or, at least, this was what he understood as a
"democratic way" of solving problems, and he was extremely
anxious to learn the tricks of democratic statesmanship at
that stage.

As his closest associates later explained to me, it took them
two months to persuade him to quit the Party in 1990 at the
28th Party Congress when hundreds of thousands across the
country were already doing that without slightest hesitation.
And it took them no less time to persuade him to lead the
country into confrontation with the regime. But, once the
hesitations were over, he performed with style and forceful-
ness in both cases. His appearance on television in February
1991 and his "declaration of war on the government" galva-
nized the country. By March practically all coal mines were
paralyzed by strikes, while massive demonstrations in
Moscow and other large cities were growing every day. A
new momentum was given to the movement when half a
million Moscovites defied the ban on demonstrations de-
spite a display of military force. Even 50,000 of the best
Army troops summoned to Moscow could not scare them
any longer. After that, the tidal wave of revolution seemed
to be unstoppable. By April the whole of Byelorussia went

on strike. It was a nation which was not previously known for its rebellious spirit, and all indications were in evidence that the Ukraine was about to follow the suit. Clearly, the country was ready to break the shackles of communism and was indeed eager to do so. All it needed was a leader of national stature who was equally determined to lead it into battle.

This was a crucial moment in our history, one which will be studied by scholars in the years to come. For the first time in almost seventy-five years of ruthless communist *diktat*, the Russian population was openly challenging it in a nonviolent but determined way. This popular impulse alone, uniting, as it were, all nations and social groups of the vast country, was priceless in itself, for only those who regain their dignity can build a new society. No true recovery is possible for the downtrodden without such a moral victory, no true democracy can emerge unless they liberate themselves.

Moreover, oppositional structures, weak and inexperienced as they were after seventy-five years of repression, could grow into a real political force capable of displacing *nomenklatura* at all levels only as a result of a struggle in the process of confrontation with the old regime. Only then, as experience shows, does the logic of struggle restructure the whole fabric of the society, bringing forward the most capable organizers, the true leaders of the people, in every district and at every workplace. Only then is there a genuine political alternative. This is how nations are reborn. Without this process, there can be no structural support for new democratic power and, therefore, there can be no systemic change in a country.

In short, if we only had a true leader at that crucial moment of our history, the fate of Russia would have been quite different. All the difficulties of transition notwithstanding, we would have been well on the road to recovery, much like Eastern Europe. Alas, there was no such leader.

Just as the things were coming to a head in April of 1991, Yeltsin lost heart and made a compromise with Gorbachev, later known as the "Novo-Ogarievo deal," thus dumping the people's fighting spirit, defusing the tension, and actually betraying his most faithful followers, the coal miners.

Worse than that, instead of relying on the people and making a clean break with the past, he allied himself with the "liberal" part of *nomenklatura*, thus creating what was later called a "center-left coalition"—the main reason for his inability to introduce much-needed reforms after August. Ironically, in doing this he promoted and strengthened his future "grave-diggers," nominated his future enemy, Alexander Rutskoi, to be his running mate in the presidential elections, and forced the reluctant Supreme Soviet to elect yet another future enemy, Ruslan Khazbulatov, as its chairman. He was reduced to a mere figurehead, but he had no one to blame but himself. Those who mistrust the people should not play politics in time of a national crisis.

However, in all fairness to Yeltsin, we must add that, although his was definitely a decisive voice, he was by no means the only one scared by the prospect of confrontation in April. Most of the "democrats" as well as a sizable number of Moscow intellectuals, were scared, too. Only a few dared to publicly advocate a call for general strike or a campaign of civil disobedience. The rest were faking prudence, pointing out the danger of provoking a crackdown (as if it had not already started in January), or a military coup with its inevitable bloodbath, or even arguing—typically for intellectuals—that the *people* were not ready to answer such call (as if the strikes were not already spreading like wildfire). Instead, they were talking about the need to follow the Polish example of the "roundtable agreement" as if that example did not negate their own conclusion: It was a notorious mistake already recognized by the Poles themselves. Besides, at least Polish Solidarity was many millions strong, well-organized and came to the "roundtable" after surviving years of marital law. A "table" in Moscow in April of 1991 could be anything but "round."

The post-August democracy in Russia was already doomed after April, four months before it was actually born. The people were ready to fight for it, but the "elites" were not, preferring a cozy cohabitation with communists to the power of the people, by the people, for the people.

Yeltsin's First Hundred Days

Nevertheless, as if to confirm an old notion that reality is the best scriptwriter of the most improbable scenarios, fate gave them one last chance: the so called "August coup" of 1991. Here is not the place to discuss what was it and why, but for the sake of our present discussion we should simply say that it was a blessing in disguise because it precipitated collapse of the communist system.[2] One can only guess how long this demoralizing uncertainty would have dragged on otherwise, with intellectuals exercising their tongues about the wisdom off a "roundtable agreement" and the horrors of confrontation, and the West "saving" its dear friend, "Gorby." So, as if to shame them all, the Evil Empire decided to strike back and fell apart, revealing how rotten it really was.

Suddenly, there was an opportunity to make up for the past indecision, but it required a very quick and radical action while the *nomenklatura* was still shell-shocked and the team was magnificent throughout the "coup" as well as for the first few days afterwards. Undoubtedly, climbing on a tank in front of his "White House" and appealing to the country was Yeltsin's best hour, and signing a decree banning the Communist Party of the Soviet Union a few days later was the most significant act of his life. But that was it, and for the next hundred days he did absolutely nothing important as if paralyzed by his unexpected victory.

Meanwhile, this was the most crucial period. Although its backbone was broken, the old regime was still very much alive, particularly in the periphery. As in 1917, the August revolution triumphed in the center, mostly in the few large cities, while the provinces remained untouched. It happened so quickly that local bosses did not have time to reveal their support for the putsch, although more than 70 percent of them sympathized with it. On the other hand, the quick defeat of the "coup" also deprived democratic forces of time needed to consolidate and create their structures. In theory, therefore, they were bearing responsibility of a party in power, while in reality they had no power in the provinces. Yeltsin did nothing at all to promote them to power. Instead, he dispatched his personal "representative" to each district, usually a former bureaucrat who would quickly find a common language with the local bureaucracy.

But even in the center, where Yeltsin's power was initially unchallenged, it was not enough just to seal the Party's headquarters and to confiscate its property. The other parts of the totalitarianism machinery should have been dismantled as quickly as possible, including: the KGB, with its intricate system of secret agents; the monstrously oversized Army with its all too powerful industrial base; and the ministries, which still controlled every aspect of production and distribution in the country.

Above all, the very essence of the communist regime should have been completely delegitimized once and for all by a systematic exposure of its crimes, preferably in an open trial or a public inquiry in which all the relevant documents from the Party and the KGB archives could have been presented and publicized. What is more, there was no need even to invent a pretext for such an investigation, as many of the top communist leaders were already in jail awaiting a trial for their participation in the August "coup." By simply making this investigation public, in front of television cameras, and by expanding the charges against the "plotters" beyond the "coup," Yeltsin could have easily turned it into a Nuremburg-type tribunal.

The task was to finish off the old structures of power and to create the new ones, thus shifting the power from the *nomenklatura* to the people. Needless to say, it also meant ending Yeltsin's "center-left coalition" with the "liberal" part of *nomenklatura,* and that could have been achieved by new elections for the Supreme Soviet of Russia. All this, and much more, could have been easily achieved in the first hundred days after the August coup, while the terrified *nomenklatura* offered no resistance, and Yeltsin's personal popularity was at its zenith.

One would think it was only too obvious that the unexpected success of August should have been broadened and built upon while the situation was so favorable. Above all, the most painful yet unavoidable reforms should have been proclaimed right from the start: *first and foremost,* a sweeping privatization of the simplest state property, such as housing, services, retail and wholesale trade. This move alone would have significantly broadened the social base of Yeltsin's power, while establishing a key principle of private property in a country where it had been absent for nearly seventy-five years. No further market reforms were possible without introducing this principle and creating its legal basis. Besides, this would have replaced collapsing system of centralized state distribution in the country—the main reason for shortages and the main source of corruption—with normal market distribution. But it also would have provided a sizable part of the population with an instant reward, a tangible result of the revolution.

Combined with the purge of *nomenklatura* and with the reelection of the Russian legislature, this would have brought completely new people into positions of power, while removing the main obstacle to further reforms—the old legislature invented by Gorbachev in order to slow down the process of change. Instead of begging his enemies to vote themselves out of existence by adopting a new constitution and a law on privatization of land, Yeltsin could have created a new instrument of power for himself. At least, it would have made the post-August 1991 changes irreversible while significantly strengthening his position.

There was also an urgent need to extricate the country from its imperial past, and here again, Yeltsin was too hesitant if not ambiguous. Although he finally delivered a *coup de grace* to the Union in December of 1991, his vision of Russia's future role in inter-republican relations was less than clear, leaving the ground for potential conflicts. The former republics were proclaimed independent and recognized as such in Moscow, but Russia claimed to be "legal heir" of the Soviet Union, with all the responsibilities for maintaining peace in the former empire. This was a colossal blunder. Not only did it make the Russian people—the biggest and the longest suffering victims of communism—the only parties held legally responsible for communism's crimes, it also rendered impossible any significant reform of the huge Soviet armed forces, scattered as they were across the former empire, very often engaged in policing local ethnic conflicts.

Furthermore, it made the former Soviet Army a pawn in a political chess game of republican leaders, most of whom, being former communist *apparatchiks,* desperately needed to obliterate that fact from the memory of their respective nations by "standing up to Moscow" and playing on the most primitive nationalist emotions of the crowd. Hence, the natural tension between Russia and the Ukraine over Crimea and the Black Sea fleet, as well as artificial tension between Russia and Georgia over Abkhasia and with Moldova over the Trans-dniestr "republic," were encouraged to grow.

On the other hand, local warring parties of the numerous ethnic conflicts viewed the Soviet Army present there either as a source of military supplies, or as a potential ally should they manage to provoke its anger against their opponents in the conflict. More often than not, local Russian settlers would be made hostage in this cruel game, and this, in turn, fueled nationalist feelings while adding up to economic troubles in Russia by generating a stream of refugees to the mainland.

Finally, the Army commanders in the areas of the conflicts were often left to follow their own political instincts in dealing with the situation, and those instincts were not necessarily democratically-oriented. If nothing else, it was in their interest to prolong the conflicts as long as possible because it was perceived as the only guarantee against reduction of the armed forces and other unpleasant reforms.

It was clearly a recipe for disaster, a ticking time-bomb, and still is. The only solution for this potentially explosive problem would have been a refusal of the Russian leadership right from the start to be dragged into any conflicts outside of Russia, a quick withdrawal of all troops from non-Russian territories and a thorough restructuring of the armed forces. Politically, it could have been achieved only by a unilateral withdrawal of Russia from the Union right after the August coup.

Of course, this is not to say that Yeltsin could have accomplished all those reforms in the remaining few months of 1991, but he certainly could and should have launched them, thus establishing the main fundamentals of his policy. The trouble is, he did nothing at all in those first hundred days, except shifting and shuffling the old bureaucratic deck. As a result, bureaucracy multiplied and completely overtook every sphere of the government, rendering it uncontrollable and incredibly corrupt. The absence of a government-sponsored radical program of privatization only gave the new bureaucracy the chance to "privatize" in its own corrupt ways. Former Party functionaries who, of course, all turned out to be "democrats" now, quickly became "businessmen," grabbing more than their fair share of desirable state-owned properties in what was de facto "privatization." Black-market operators and outright criminals got the rest, and the most valuable property was "privatized" without benefit of the law. This, of course, generated quite a predictable public resentment and gave a bad name to the whole idea of a market economy.

It also secured a financial base for the reviving *nomenklatura*. Political paralysis in the center gave it an opportunity to re-group and to work out a new strategy, this time a completely "democratic" one. There was no need for coups and conspiracies where sabotage and subversion could do the trick, particularly as the inevitable chaos, hunger, and breakdown of law and order were bound to play into their hand by bringing social tension to a peak. Yeltsin's government, which was already rapidly losing its popularity because of its communist past and its corrupt present, could hardly be expected to survive such a course of events. All the communists needed to do under the circumstances was to act as a "democratic" opposition defending the interests of the ordinary people, while at the same time blocking or sabotaging any further reforms. Their domination of both the executive and the legislative branches of the government was already quite sufficient for winning this new game of "democracy." Their new financial power, acquired through their "private business activity," enabled them to create highly visible political structures.

Small and disunited though genuinely democratic forces could only continue to split and squabble under these circumstances and found themselves in a no-win situation. They could not openly oppose Yeltsin for fear of playing into the hand of the communists, yet they could not support him either without alienating their grass-roots followers. In the end, some joined the government, others dropped out of politics altogether, while a majority joined the ranks of the disillusioned multitudes, who felt betrayed and robbed of the fruits of their revolution.

Indeed, what else could they feel seeing exactly the same
Party bureaucrats sitting in the same offices doing the same
jobs and enjoying the same privileges as they did before
August? What else could they feel when Yeltsin and his
team, in a gesture of total disregard for popular feelings,
moved their headquarters from the White House—a symbol
of their revolution—to the former offices of the Communist
rulers in the Kremlin, while their comrades' blood still was
not quite dried up on the pavement? Which Yeltsin were
they supposed to support: the one who climbed a tank, now
and then, to declare a war on the *nomenklatura,* or the one
who advocated a compromise with it between his declara-
tions of war? Surely, one cannot be expected to do both.

Only one hundred days after its victory, Yeltsin's government looked more and more like the provisional government of 1917, with its inability to solve society's main problems, its lack of political structures, and its dwindling popularity. It failed to capitalize on a few opportunities offered
by good fortune because it was led by the wrong people who
just happened to be at the right place in the right moment.
There was nothing to hope for any longer. I wrote at the
time, in the *New York Times Magazine,* after returning from
Moscow: "The sad reality is that, seventy-four years later,
we still haven't gotten it right. While there were far too
many revolutionaries in 1917, this time there are too few."

Yegor Gaidar and His Reforms

As if all these blunders were not enough for one man to
make in a few months, Yeltsin made yet another: Without
resolving the problem of political power in the country and
without establishing the institution of private property, he
appointed Yegor Gaidar to introduce a "market economy."

Ironically, very much like Mikhail Gorbachev before him,
the new Russian star was immediately acclaimed in the West

as a young, energetic, Westernized crusader for laissez faire economics, while in reality he was the offspring of the old *nomenklatura* deadwood. His grandfather, a famous Soviet children's writer, made himself a name by glorifying the Bolshevik Revolution and the Russian Civil War; his father, a Soviet admiral, followed family tradition and glorified the bravery of the Soviet Army in Afghanistan. Needless to say, with such a prominent revolutionary pedigree, Gaidar III made a spectacular professional career in different think-tanks of the Central Committee, working on its main theoretical magazine, *Kommunist,* and later as the economics editor of *Pravda.* Incredibly, he was Yeltsin's choice as Russian Prime Minister.

Gaidar's team consisted of young, energetic liberal-minded children of the *nomenklatura* who spent their life in different prestigious research institutes. Undoubtedly, under Brezhnev, they were even perceived as somewhat rebellious for trying to persuade the old dogmatic Central Committee that socialism needed to incorporate some elements of market economy. I suspect they may have even read Milton Friedman, Ludwig von Mises, and Friedrich von Hayek secretly while students. The trouble was, however, that their knowledge of economic life was rather bookish, as they never lived lives as ordinary humans under socialism or capitalism.

Be that as it may, these "radical reformers" persuaded Yeltsin to adopt the Polish model of "shock therapy," and to start the whole process with "liberalization of prices." Right from the beginning of 1992 they did so, in a firm belief that, combined with tight monetary and fiscal policies, this measure would enable them to make the ruble convertible by summer and privatization possible by the fall.

The result was catastrophe. The "reforms" welcomed in the West as "courageous" in reality were downright stupid, because they totally ignored a colossal difference between the Russian and Polish economies. Polish agriculture was never collectivized and was always based on private farming. Private services and retail and wholesale trade already existed for decades before "shock therapy." Russia had no private farmers, producers, or traders, and no private sector whatsoever. It did not even have a legal basis for private property. Accordingly, while "shock therapy" in Poland stimulated competition in the private sector, (employing about one-third of the total workforce), and, therefore, after an initial jump of some 60 percent, prices stabilized within a few months, prices in Russia jumped *20 times,* and continued to grow. In the absence of a private sector and with shortages of consumer goods as common as ever, there was no competition to be stimulated: Monopolistic producers could safely reduce their production and fix the prices at any level. Needless to say, production dropped 20-30 percent everywhere, including in agriculture.

At the same time, Gaidar's "tight monetary and fiscal policies"—after all, he learned something from Friedman's books—severely discouraged any private initiative. With income taxes on a Swedish scale, (federal and local taxes combined could reach 90 percent), and an absence of cheap credits, any enthusiast of a private business activity was promptly driven underground, where shady deals were made only in cash (to the utter delight of the racketeers). Naturally, this "business activity" could never go beyond simple profiteering in an atmosphere of bureaucratic corruption, raging inflation, high taxes and racketeering. No one would be so crazy as to "invest" into any production in such circumstances, particularly in a country with no laws on private property.

Consequently, private initiative was directed into wasteful activity instead of being harnessed to develop a market economy: It did not accumulate capital, engage in competition, or create new jobs and new products. It did not even contribute its share to the general revenue, but it did fuel inflation, crime, and a popular hatred of "ugly capitalism."

Meanwhile, unlike in Poland, the bulk of Russian industry was not consumer-oriented, but state-controlled "heavy industry," some 30-40 percent of which was related to military production. Any market reform in the country was bound to affect it dramatically, generating a huge wave of unemployment. Now, since no government can survive unemployment of such proportions, least of all as feeble a government as Yeltsin's, market reforms in Russia were possible only with a very rapid development of the private sector, capable of creating new jobs. Even that might have been insufficient, and a program of public works, like the one under FDR in the United States, should have been prepared.

But neither was conceived. Suddenly, a combination of Gaidar's "tight monetarism" of staggering inflation and of the underground "cash economy" resulted in a liquidity crisis, or, as it was officially termed in Russia, a "crisis of payment." To put it in plain language, the Russian economy went bankrupt: No one could pay anyone because of a lack of cash. Enterprises could not pay for raw materials, for energy, for services, for products provided by connected enterprises; workers were not paid their wages for several months. Mutual debts piled up and reached a total of several trillion rubles, while only few years before, in 1989, the entire national income of the then Soviet Union was assessed at under one trillion rubles.

Fortunately for all involved, there were no laws on bankruptcy either—the Congress of People's Deputies previously refused to adopt any—or the government would have had to deal with 30-40 million unemployed and very angry people. Still, there were a few hair-raising moments, such as when a nuclear weapons factory in Siberia went on strike, and Yeltsin personally had to bring the workers money in his plane in order to pay their overdue wages.

But this was the end of Gaidar's "reform." By the summer

of 1992, instead of the promised convertible ruble, the government had to print the ordinary one in astronomic numbers. Under pressure from furious legislators, the government also had to re-establish massive subsidies of industry and periodic indexation of wages and pensions. It restored Gorbachev's old economic "policy" of the printing press and of begging additional credits in the West. To be sure, there was still plenty of talk about reforms and even a half-hearted attempt at "privatization" in the fall, "as planned." Indeed, the "Privatization Cheques," or "vouchers" as they are more commonly known in Russia, with a face value of 10,000 rubles each, were duly printed and distributed to every Russian citizen. But the popular response was lukewarm: No one knew what sort of the state property would be available for "vouchers." Would it be something useful, like land or housing, or would it be a tiny piece of a gigantic and rusty factory, which would never be profitable? Meanwhile, the "vouchers" simply added yet another trillion or so rubles to an already uncontrollable rate of inflation as they went into circulation and became legal tender in Russia.

"Market reform" ended in Russia, leaving people twenty times poorer, more disillusioned and more angry. It could not serve the communists better: While the country still had neither democracy, nor a market economy, both ideas were utterly discredited. The outrageous robbery of Yeltsin's first one hundred days completely obliterated from the people's memory the crimes and oppression of the previous seventy-five years. Encouraged, the *nomenklatura* went onto the offensive, gradually forcing Yeltsin, first, to abandon his policies, then, to sacrifice his team, and, finally, to fight for his own political survival while his constant vacillations between confrontation and compromise only decreased his popularity.

Is There Hope for Russia?

Clearly, new forces, new people—preferably, a new generation—must come to the Russian political scene, if the
country is to survive. Yet, there are no new forces, and the
existing ones are not strong enough to resolve the crisis.
This is exactly the reason why the most commonly suggested
scenarios of the Russian future—the Bolshevik coup of 1917
type, the Weimar Republic with a new Hitler emerging out
of its chaos type, the military coup of the Pinochet type or
an all-out Civil War type as in the former Yugoslavia—are
not likely to happen. For if there were forces capable of
carrying out any of the above scenarios, they would have
won long ago, or, at least, they would have manifested themselves in a convincing way. For instance, look at the present-
day "Bolsheviks" and at all of yesterday's *apparatchiks:* Are
they eager to take upon themselves the responsibility of absolute power? Far from it; they prefer Yeltsin and his lot to
bear responsibility, while they line their pockets. And how
many followers do they have in the country, if even at the
time of a profound economic crisis and misery they could
hardly gather a 100,000-strong demonstration in Moscow?

Or, let us look at the Russian "nationalists," so much publicized in the West as if they were just about to storm the
Kremlin. Where are their "black hundreds"? In all these
years of turmoil and with all the trappings of a Weimar
Republic in evidence, they failed to get a single deputy
elected even to a local Soviet anywhere in the country in the
early 1990s. In fact, they were hardly more numerous than
the skinheads in any European country. This is why they
had to ally themselves with the communists in what became
known as a "brown-red coalition": both partners of this un-
happy marriage knew they were too weak to survive alone.

Military dictatorship is even a less likely scenario. Long
gone are the days when the Army was a monolithic force,
forged by discipline into an iron fist of the Party. Today's

Russian Army is a force only in name. It is torn by its internal problems and conflicts. The conscripts want to go home; the junior officers want better housing and salaries; the generals want to play soldiers who, in turn, want to go home. Add ethnic conflicts, corruption, abuse, and total political confusion, like anywhere else in the country, and the emerging picture is a one of a liability rather than of an all-powerful force.

Besides, none of the above mentioned "forces" has the slightest idea how to solve the country's problems. Their usual demagoguery apart, even the communists know there is no way back to five-year plans and campaigns of "socialist competition." Even the most extreme nationalists know that there is no way back to the Soviet empire without a prolonged and bloody war for which Russia has no strength. And, after bungling their reforms, the democrats have no clear answers either.

Meanwhile, as political paralysis in the center continues, with tiny groups of politicians in Moscow being deadlocked in their squabbles, and with the government printing more and more money, the provinces are very likely to look for their own solutions. In fact, fragmentation of Russia proper has already started, and not necessarily along ethnic lines. Some districts, in their desperate quest for stability, have introduced local "currency" as a buffer against an inflationary ruble; others have openly contemplated a separation from the Russian Federation. Perhaps this is as it should be in a state that has been historically built from top to bottom rather than from the bottom to the top. Perhaps there is no other solution for a country where the development of local self-government has been prevented for nearly seventy-five years. Indeed, can anyone explain why Siberia, or the Far East, while still fabulously rich in resources, should continue to suffer just because nine time-zones away in a far-off Moscow some fools are squabbling over obscure constitutional subtleties? What did Moscow ever give to them, except orders, plans demands, punishment, taxation, and now hyperinflation?

Undoubtedly, a drive for "sovereignty" was the most powerful force of the current Russian revolution, and not only among different ethnic groups. In fact, it might have been the only popular concept of freedom in the over-centralized totalitarian state—a desire to be separated from it by some kind of a border, preferably by an iron curtain. This, and not a handful of former communists-turned-democrats, effectively finished off totalitarian control, thus making the country ungovernable. The idea of a self-sacrifice for a common good has been so over-exploited under socialism that it has produced a powerful backlash. In a country, where everyone has been an employee of the state, a bureaucrat of a sort, the universal dream has been to become a boss of one's own. And, if my guess is correct, no common idea or common cause can unite them until they fulfill this dream, ruin the country, and again learn to voluntarily subordinate themselves to a common interest. This will be the most difficult lesson of democracy they have yet to learn.

In the meantime, we should brace ourselves for all sorts of disasters. Clearly, even large fragments of the former Soviet empire will not be able to maintain a national infrastructure in communications, transportation, and energy, to say nothing of maintaining the safety of nuclear and chemical industries. There is also little likelihood of maintaining the Academy of Science with its research institutes, and the artistic culture that has arisen over hundreds of years. In fact, Russia may be thrown two centuries back, into the age of horse-power, with its entire intellectual potential being completely lost.

Furthermore, we cannot predict how the fragments of Russia are going to be governed: by elected parliaments or by warlords? Will they live peacefully with each other, or will they fight for oil fields and gold resources? And, if they fight, what sort of weapons will they use?

Questions like these are as yet unanswerable. The biggest among them is: What can we do about it? Even today, the West can do next to nothing, no matter how much it wants to "help Yeltsin." A few billion dollars more is not going to make much difference, particularly as most of this sum will be embezzled by the corrupt Russian bureaucracy anyway. But when the country disintegrates, we will be even less able to help it.

So, what can we do? Is there hope for Russia? Yes. But it rests with the younger generation, which so far has remained largely inactive and apolitical. This is without precedent in the world's history. Most of them are so mistrustful of their elders that the overwhelming majority—some 70 percent according to opinion polls, wants simply to emigrate. Unless we find a way to wake them up, to give them hope, there will be no hope for Russia.

Notes

[1] *The Statesman's Year-Book, 1988–1989;* 125th edition (New York: Macmillan Reference Books), 1217.

[2] I refer those who are interested in a more detailed analysis of the August 1991 "coup" to my article, "The Disappearing Act," published in *The New Republic,* January 6-13, 1992.

Ludwig von Mises

Readings 1 and 2: "The Impracticability of Socialism" and "Observations on the Russian Reform Movement"

Editor's Note: Ludwig von Mises was recognized as the leading figure of the Austrian School of economics in the 20th century. Born in 1881, Mises graduated from the University of Vienna in 1906. He worked as a senior economic analyst for the Austrian Chamber of Commerce from 1907 until 1934, when he moved to Geneva, Switzerland, where he assumed a position as Professor of International Economic Relations at the Graduate Institute for International Studies. Mises came to the United States in 1940. He was a visiting professor in the Graduate School for Business Administration at New York University from 1945 until 1969. Mises also served as director of the League of Nations' Austrian Reparations Commission (1918–1920) and was the founder (in 1927) and first vice-president of the Austrian Institute for Economic Research. He died in 1973.

Among his most important works are The Theory of Money and Credit *(1912),* Nation, State, and Economy *(1919),* Socialism, An Economic and Sociological Analysis *(1922),* Liberalism *(1927),* Critique of Interventionism *(1929),* Epistemological Problems of Economics *(1933),* Omnipotent Government *(1944),* Bureaucracy *(1944),* Human Action, A Treatise on Economics *(1949),* Planning for Freedom *(1952),* The Anti-Capitalistic Mentality *(1956),* Theory and

History *(1957)*, The Ultimate Foundations of Economic Science *(1962) and* The Historical Setting of the Austrian School of Economics *(1969)*.

In 1920, Mises published an essay on, "Economic Calculation in the Socialist Commonwealth," in which he demonstrated that the elimination of private property, competitive markets and money prices for both consumer goods and factors of production would lead to economic irrationality. The central planners of a nationalized economy would have no method for efficient, least-cost allocation of resources among alternative productive uses. The end result would be "planned chaos" and societal poverty and decay. As Mises expressed it in 1922, "Socialism ... is not the pioneer of a better and finer world, but the spoiler of what thousands of years of civilization have created. It does not build, it destroys. For destruction is the essence of it. It produces nothing, it only consumes what the social order based on private ownership in the means of production has created."

The first excerpt here, "The Impracticability of Socialism," in which Mises summarizes his criticisms of socialist central planning, is taken from Liberalism *(1927). The second excerpt, "Observations on the Russian Reform Movement," originally appeared in* The Freeman *(May, 1966) and explains why attempts to reform the socialist economy in Soviet Russia were bound to fail. Mises concluded that only a comprehensive return to a fully privatized, free market could reverse the disasters produced by central planning.*

"The Impracticability of Socialism"*

People are wont to consider socialism impracticable because they think that men lack the moral qualities demanded by a socialist society. It is feared that under socialism most men will not exhibit the same zeal in the perfor-

---

*Reprinted from *Liberalism in the Classical Tradition* (Foundation for Economic Education and Cobden Press, 1985).

mance of the duties and tasks assigned to them that they bring to their daily work in a social order based on private ownership of the means of production. In a capitalist society, every individual knows that the fruit of his labor is his own to enjoy, that his income increases or decreases according as the output of his labor is greater or smaller. In a socialist society, every individual will think that less depends on the efficiency of his own labor, since a fixed portion of the total output is due him in any case and the amount of the latter cannot be appreciably diminished by the loss resulting from the laziness of any one man. If, as is to be feared, such a conviction should become general, the productivity of labor in a socialist community would drop considerably.

The objection thus raised against socialism is completely sound, but it does not get to the heart of the matter. Were it possible in a socialist community to ascertain the output of the labor of every individual comrade with the same precision with which this is accomplished for each worker by means of economic calculation in the capitalist system, the practicability of socialism would not be dependent on the good will of every individual. Society would be in a position, at least within certain limits, to determine the share of the total output to be allotted to each worker on the basis of the extent of his contribution to production. What renders socialism impracticable is precisely the fact that calculation of this kind is impossible in a socialist society.

In the capitalist system, the calculation of profitability constitutes a guide that indicates to the individual whether the enterprise he is operating ought, under the given circumstances, to be in operation at all and whether it is being run in the most efficient possible way, i.e., at the least cost in factors of production. If an undertaking proves unprofitable, this means that the raw materials, half-finished goods, and labor that are needed in it are employed by other enterprises for an end that, from the standpoint of the consumers, is more urgent and more important, or for the same end, but in a more economical manner (i.e., with a smaller expenditure of capital and labor). When, for instance, hand weaving came to be unprofitable, this signified that the capital and labor employed in weaving by machine yield a greater output and that it is consequently uneconomical to adhere to a method of production in which the same input of capital and labor yields a smaller output.

If a new enterprise is being planned, one can calculate in advance whether it can be made profitable at all and in what way. If, for example, one has the intention of constructing a railroad line, one can, by estimating the traffic to be expected and its ability to pay the freight rates, calculate whether it pays to invest capital and labor in such an undertaking. If the result of this calculation shows that the projected railroad promises no profit, this is tantamount to saying that there is other, more urgent employment for the capital and the labor that the construction of the railroad would require; the world is not yet rich enough to be able to afford such an expenditure. But it is not only when the question arises whether or not a given undertaking is to be begun at all that the calculation of value and profitability is decisive; it controls every single step that the entrepreneur takes in the conduct of his business.

Capitalist economic calculation, which alone makes rational production possible, is based on monetary calculation. Only because the prices of all goods and services in the market can be expressed in terms of money is it possible for them, in spite of their heterogeneity, to enter into a calculation involving homogeneous units of measurement. In a socialist society, where all the means of production are owned by the community, and where, consequently, there is no market and no exchange of productive goods and services, there can also be no money prices for goods and services of higher order. Such a social system would thus, of necessity, be lacking in the means for the rational management of business enterprises, viz., economic calculation. For economic calculation cannot take place in the absence of a common denominator to which all the heterogeneous goods and services can be reduced.

Let us consider a quite simple case. For the construction of a railroad from A to B several routes are conceivable. Let us suppose that a mountain stands between A and B. The railroad can be made to run over the mountain, around the mountain, or, by way of a tunnel, through the mountain. In a capitalist society, it is a very easy matter to compute which line will prove the most profitable. One ascertains the cost involved in constructing each of the three lines and the differences in operating costs necessarily incurred by the anticipated traffic on each. From these quantities it is not difficult to determine which stretch of road will be the most profitable. A socialist society could not make such calculations. For it would have no possible way of reducing to a uniform standard of measurement all the heterogeneous quantities and qualities of goods and services that here come into consideration. In the face of the ordinary, everyday problems which the management of an economy presents, a socialist society would stand helpless, for it would have no possible way of keeping its accounts.

The prosperity that has made it possible for many more people to inhabit the earth today than in the precapitalist era is due solely to the capitalist method of lengthy chains of production, which necessarily requires monetary calculation. This is impossible under socialism. In vain have socialist writers labored to demonstrate how one could still manage even without monetary and price calculation. All their efforts in this respect have met with failure.

The leadership of a socialist society would thus be confronted by a problem that it could not possibly solve. It would not be able to decide which of the innumerable possible modes of procedure is the most rational. The resulting chaos in the economy would culminate quickly and irresistibly in universal impoverishment and a retrogression to the primitive conditions under which our ancestors once lived.

The socialist ideal, carried to its logical conclusion, would eventuate in a social order in which all the means of production were owned by the people as a whole. Production would be completely in the hands of the government, the center of power in society. It alone would determine what was to be produced and how, and in what way goods ready for consumption were to be distributed. It makes little difference whether we imagine this socialist state of the future as democratically constituted or otherwise. Even a democratic socialist state would necessarily constitute a tightly organized bureaucracy in which everyone, apart from the highest officials, though he might very well, in his capacity as a voter, have participated in some fashion in framing the directives issued by the central authority, would be in the subservient position of an administrator bound to carry them out obediently.

A socialist state of this kind is not comparable to the state enterprises, no matter how vast their scale, that we have seen developing in the last decades in Europe, especially in Germany and Russia. The latter all flourish *side by side with* private ownership of the means of production. They engage in commercial transactions with enterprises that capitalists own and manage, and they receive various stimuli from these enterprises that invigorate their own operation. State railroads, for instance, are provided by their suppliers, the manufacturers of locomotives, coaches, signal installations, and other equipment, with apparatus that has proved successful elsewhere in the operation of privately owned railroads. Thence they receive the incentive to institute innovations in order to keep up with the progress in technology and in methods of business management that is taking place all around them.

It is a matter of common knowledge that national and

municipal enterprises have, on the whole, failed, that they are expensive and inefficient, and that they have to be subsidized out of tax funds just to maintain themselves in operation. Of course, where a public enterprise occupies a monopolistic position—as is, for instance, generally the case with municipal transportation facilities and electric light and power plants—the bad consequences of inefficiency need not always express themselves in visible financial failure. Under certain circumstances it may be possible to conceal it by making use of the opportunity open to the monopolist of raising the price of his products and services high enough to render these enterprises, in spite of their uneconomic management, still profitable. The lower productivity of the socialist method of production merely manifests itself differently here and is not so easily recognized as otherwise; essentially, however, the case remains the same.

But none of these experiments in the socialist management of enterprises can afford us any basis for judging what it would mean if the socialist ideal of the communal ownership of *all* means of production were to be realized. In the socialist society of the future, which will leave no room whatsoever for the free activity of private enterprises operating side by side with those owned and controlled by the state, the central planning board will lack entirely the gauge provided for the whole economy by the market and market prices. In the market, where all goods and services come to be traded, exchange ratios, expressed in money prices, may be determined for everything bought and sold. In a social order based on private property, it thus becomes possible to resort to monetary calculation in checking on the results of all economic activities. The social productivity of every economic transaction may be tested by the methods of bookkeeping and cost accounting. It yet remains to be shown that public enterprises are unable to make use of cost accounting in the same way as private enterprises do. Nevertheless, monetary calculation does give even governmental and communal enterprises some basis for judging the success or failure of their management. In a completely socialist economic system, this would be quite impossible, for in the absence of private ownership of the means of production, there could be no exchange of capital goods in the market and consequently neither money prices nor monetary calculation. The general management of a purely socialist society will therefore have no means of reducing to a common denominator the costs of production of all the heterogeneous commodities that it plans to produce.

Nor can this be achieved by setting expenditures in kind against savings in kind. One cannot calculate if it is not possible to reduce to a common medium of expression hours of labor of various grades, iron, coal, building materials of every kind, machines, and all the other things needed in the operation and management of different enterprises. Calculation is possible only when one is able to reduce to monetary terms all the goods under consideration. Of course, monetary calculation has its imperfections and deficiencies, but we have nothing better to put in its place. It suffices for the practical purposes of life as long as the monetary system is sound. If we were to renounce monetary calculation, every economic computation would be come absolutely impossible.

This is the decisive objection that economics raises against the possibility of a socialist society. It must forgo the intellectual division of labor that consists in the cooperation of all entrepreneurs, landowners, and workers as producers and consumers in the formation of market prices. But without it, rationality, i.e., the possibility of economic calculation, is unthinkable.

"Observations on the Russian Reform Movement"*

The bosses of the Russian Communist Administration are disturbed by the fact that economic conditions in the countries which have not adopted the methods of the Communist International are by far more satisfactory than those in their own country. If they could succeed in keeping their "comrades" in complete ignorance of the achievements of Western capitalism, they would not mind the low efficiency of their own plants and farms. But as some scanty information about the "affluence" of the West penetrates to Russia, its masters are upset by the fear of the pro-capitalist reaction in their own house. This fear impels them on the one hand to foment sedition all over the "capitalist sector" of the earth, and on the other hand to ventilate various projects aiming at some minor reforms in their own methods of management.

Nobody is today more firmly convinced of the incomparable superiority of the capitalistic methods of production than the "production tsars" of the countries behind the Iron Curtain. The present-day strength of communism is entirely due to the mentality of the pseudo-intellectuals in the Western nations who still enjoy the products of free enterprise.

I

The market economy—capitalism—is a social system of consumers' supremacy. There is in its frame only one method of earning a living and of acquiring property, viz., one must try to serve one's fellow men, the consumers, in the best possible way. A daily and hourly repeated plebiscite determines again and again every individual's earning and

*Reprinted from *Money, Method, and the Market Process: Essays by Ludwig von Mises* (Praxeology Press, 1990).

place in society. By their buying and abstention from buying the consumers allocate ownership of all the material factors of production to those who have succeeded in satisfying the most urgent of their not yet satisfied wants in the best possible and cheapest way. Ownership of the material factors of production can be acquired and can be preserved only by serving the consumers better than other people do. It is a revocable public mandate as it were.

The supremacy of the consumers is no less complete with regard to labor, the human factor of production. Wage rates are determined by the price the consumer, in buying the product, is prepared to refund to the employer for the worker's contribution to the process of its production. Thus the consumers' valuation fixes the height of every worker's remuneration.[1] And let us not forget: The immense majority of the consumers are themselves earners of salaries and wages and in this capacity instrumental in the determination of their own compensation.

The unique efficiency of the capitalistic system is due to the incentive it gives to everybody to exert his forces to the utmost in serving his fellow citizens. Not a vague altruism, but rightly understood selfishness impels a man to put forth all his strength in the service of his fellow men. The system of economic calculation in terms of money, the commonly used medium of exchange, makes it possible to compute precisely all projects in advance and the result of every action performed in retrospect, and, what is no less important, to ascribe to every factor the size of its contribution to the outcome.

The characteristic feature of socialism is precisely the fact that it substitutes for this market system of consumers' supremacy a dictatorial system, the "plan." In the planned economy the individuals are not driven by the desire to improve their own conditions but either by dutifulness or by the fear of punishment. It is impossible for the individual workers to improve their own exertion, they alone are burdened by the implied sacrifices, but only an infinitesimal fraction of the product of their additional exertion will benefit themselves. On the other hand they can enjoy in full the pleasures of carelessness and laziness in the performances of the tasks assigned to them while the resulting impairment of the total national product curtails their own share only infinitesimally.

The economists always pointed to this inherent deficiency of socialism. Today all people in the socialist countries know that this criticism was fully justified. All their projects for an improvement of the quality and an increase in the quantity of economic goods and services turn around this problem. They all aim—unfortunately in vain—at discovering a scheme that could make the individual members of a socialist system self-interested in the effect of their own contribution to the collective's effort.

That the socialists acknowledge this fact and are anxious to find a solution amounts in itself already to a spectacular refutation of two of the most zealously advanced arguments in favor of socialism. On the one hand, the socialists asserted that in the market economy that the wage earners are not interested in improving the output of their own work. They expected that socialism would bring about an unprecedented improvement of the individual worker's contributions because everybody will be incited by the knowledge that he does not labor for an exploiter but works for his own best interest. On the other hand, the socialists vilified profit-seeking as the most pernicious and "socially" injurious institution and indulged in reveries about the blessings of what they called a substitution of "production for use" for "production for profit."

No less significant an admission of the viciousness of the socialist ideology is provided by the small plots the exploitation of which for the account of the rural workers (falsely labelled for "private profit") alone prevented famines in the country that includes a good deal of the world's most fertile arable soil. The urgency of the Soviet productivity problem is due to the fact that in the processing industries no analogous expedient is at hand.

II

The must discussed reform projects of Professor Liberman[2] and other Russian authors do not refer to the essential characteristics of the Soviet system of central planning of all activities commonly called economic. Neither do they deal in any way with the problem of economic calculation. (For present-day Russian planners this problem does not yet have primary importance as, operating within a world of the price system, they are in a position to rely upon the prices determined on the markets of the West.)

What the reformers want to attain is improvement in the conduct of factories and workshops turning out consumers' goods by the adoption of new methods for the remuneration of directors, supervisors or foremen. The salaries of such people should henceforth be meted out in such a way that they should have a pecuniary interest in producing articles that are considered as satisfactory by the consumers.

It is a serious blunder to employ in dealing with this issue any reference to the concept of "profit" or to declare that the suggested method of payment would mean something like "profit-sharing." There is within a socialist system no room for the establishment and computation of a magnitude that could be called profit or loss.

The task of production is to utilize the available human and material factors of production for the best possible satisfaction of future wants concerning which there cannot be any *certain* knowledge today.

Technology indicates for what purposes the various factors of production could be employed; it thus shows goals that could be attained provided this is considered as desirable. To choose from this bewildering multitude of possible ways of production those which most likely are fit to satisfy the most urgent of the future wants of the consumers is in the market economy the specific task of the entrepreneur. If all entrepreneurs were right in their appreciation of the future state of the market, the prices of various complementary factors of production would already have today attained the height corresponding to this future state. As, under these conditions, no entrepreneurs would have acquired some or all of the complementary factors of production at prices lower or higher than those which later events proved to be the correct ones, no profits or losses could emerge.

One profits by having expended less than one—later—receives from the buyers of the product, and one loses if one can sell only at prices that do not cover the costs expended in production. What determines profit or loss is choosing the goal to be set for the entrepreneurial activities and choosing the methods for its attainment.

Thus it is investment that results either in profit or in loss. As in a socialist system only "society" invests, only society can profit or suffer losses. But in a socialist system the material factors of production are *res extra commercium*. That means: They can neither be bought nor sold and thus no prices for them are determined. Therefore it is impossible to find out whether a definite production activity resulted in profit or loss.

The eminence of capitalism consists precisely in the fact that it tends to put the direction of production into the hands of those entrepreneurs who have best succeeded in providing for the demands of the consumers. In the planned economy such a built-in process of selection is lacking. There it does not matter whether the planning authorities have erred or not. The consumers have to take what the authorities offer them. Errors committed by the planning authority do not become known because there is no method to discover them.

In the market economy the emergency of profit demon-
strates that in the eyes of the consumers one entrepreneur
served them better than others did. Profit and loss are thus
the effect of comparing and gauging different suppliers'
performance. In the socialist system there is nothing available to make possible a comparison between the commodities fabricated and the services rendered by the plan and its
executors with something originating from another side.
The behavior of the people for whom the plan and its executors are supposed to provide does not indicate whether
or not a better method of providing for their needs would
have been feasible. If in dealing with socialism one speaks
of profits, one merely creates confusion. There are no profits outside the "profit and loss system."

If the authorities promise to the director of a shoe factory
a bonus to be determined as a percentage of sales, they do
not give him a share in "profits." Still less can it be called a
return to the profit system. Profits can only be calculated if
one deducts total costs from total receipts. Any such operation is unfeasible under the conditions of the case. The
whole factory, fully equipped, was handed over by the
authorities to the care of the director and with it all the
material needed and the order, to produce, with the help
of workers assigned to the outfit, a definite quantity of foot-
wear for delivery to definite shops. There is no method
available to find out the costs incurred by all the operations
preceding the first interference of the director. The bonus
granted to him cannot have any relation to the numerical
difference between such total costs and the proceeds from
the sale of the final product.

III

In fact the problem of reform as today passionately discussed in the communist countries does not deal with the
profitability of the various plants and productive processes.

It turns virtually around a different problem: Is it possible within a socialist system to remunerate a worker, especially also the supreme foreman of a plant, according to the value the consumers, the people, attach to his contribution to the accomplishment of the product or the service?

In the capitalistic or market economy the employer is bound to pay a hired worker the price the consumers are prepared to refund to him in buying the product. If he were to pay more, he would suffer losses, would forfeit his funds and would be eliminated from the ranks of the entrepreneurs. If he tried to pay less, the competition of other employers would make it impossible for him to find helpers. Under socialism no such connection between the amounts expended in the production of a commodity and its appreciation by the consumers prevails. There cannot therefore *in general* be any question of remunerating workers according to their "productivity" as appreciated by the consumers. Only in exceptional cases is it possible to separate the contribution of one worker in such a way from those of all other contributors that its separate valuation by the consumers and therefore its remuneration according to this valuation become feasible. For instance: all seats in the opera house can be sold at the regular price of m. But if a tenor of world fame sings the main part, the house is sold out even if the price of admission is raised to $m + n$. It is obvious that such cases are extremely rare and must not be referred to in dealing with the problem of wage rate determination under socialism.

Of course, a socialist management can determine for many kinds of work "normal" tasks to be performed by the laborer and on the one hand reward those who accomplish more and on the other hand penalize those who fail to produce their quotas. But such a norm in no way depends on any market phenomena. It is the outcome of a more or less arbitrary decision of the authorities.

In the market economy the salaries paid to people who

turn out commodities or render services that cannot be sold on the market and for which therefore no prices are available are indirectly determined by the structure of the market. The employer—in such cases as a rule the government—must pay to such people enough to prevent them from preferring a job in the orbit of the market. Such indirect determination of the height of wage rates, too, is unfeasible in a socialist system.

Of course, the government is always free to grant to any of the officials it employs a salary equal to the value the supreme chief or planner attaches to this man's services. But this does not have any reference to the social problem around which the discussion turns.

Notes

[1]This is to what the jargon of the Hollywood industry refers in using the term "box office account." But it is no less valued for all other fields of business.

[2][Yevsei Liberman in the 1960s began writing in the Soviet Union that profits should be the "the index of the efficiency of an enterprise." In 1966 a plan was instituted granting autonomy to 43 different enterprises in various industries. The result was an increase in productivity and worker income, leading to greater individual savings and more exportable goods. See *Socialism: The Grand Delusion*, Brian Crozier and Arthur Seldon, eds. (New York: Universe Books, 1986), 138–39. The plan was an embarrassing success for the advocates of state socialism— Ed.]